# WHY BLAME THE ORGANIZATION?

# WHY BLAME THE ORGANIZATION?

## A Pragmatic Analysis of
## Collective Moral Responsibility

Raymond S. Pfeiffer

LITTLEFIELD ADAMS BOOKS

LITTLEFIELD ADAMS BOOKS

Published in the United States of America
by Rowman & Littlefield Publishers, Inc.
4720 Boston Way, Lanham, Maryland 20706

3 Henrietta Street
London WC2E 8LU, England

Most of chapter five was originally published in the *Journal of Business Ethics*, vol. 9:
473-480, 1990 as "The Central Distinction in the Theory of Corporate Moral
Personhood." © 1990 Kluwer Academic Publishers. Printed in the Netherlands.
Reprinted by permission of Kluwer Academic Publishers.

British Cataloging in Publication Information Available

**Library of Congress Cataloging-in-Publication Data**

Pfeiffer, Raymond S.
Why blame the organization? : a pragmatic analysis of collective moral responsibility /
by Raymond S. Pfeiffer.
p. cm.
Includes bibliographical references and index.
1. Organizational sociology. 2. Organizational behavior—Moral and ethical aspects. 3.
Responsibility. 4. Blame. I. Title.
HM131.P425   1995   302.3'5—dc20     95–33952     CIP
ISBN 0–8226–3044-3 (cloth : alk. paper)
ISBN 0–8226–3045-1 (pbk. : alk. paper)

Printed in the United States of America

☉™ The paper used in this publication meets the minimum requirements of
American National Standard for Information Sciences—Permanence of
Paper for Printed Library Materials, ANSI Z39.48–1984.

For LoLita, Mariah, Ryan, and Caven

# CONTENTS

# Preface

Organizations are perhaps the most powerful and effective inventions of the human race. Developments in technology and culture have brought increasing variety, complexity, and power to economic, political, and social organizations of all kinds. It is through organizations that most power is wielded in the contemporary world.

Organizations simultaneously augment the power of individuals and limit their freedom. Organizations, however, do not entirely eclipse individuality, as they are still the instruments of individuals. Much in contemporary culture reminds us daily that individuals are what matter most.

Wealthy and powerful individuals are, of course, the favorites of the mass media. Their achievements, foibles, and failures are sources of endless public amusement, wonder, and controversy. This may reassure some that in the end, individuals are supreme, that one may rise above the din, and that there is the potential for greatness, even if only through wealth, fame, or power.

Even for the rich and famous, however, most of life progresses within the boundaries of social, political, and economic organizations. To gain or hold power and wealth in contemporary society requires success at working in and through organizations. In many respects, our society rewards with individual freedom those who offer skills and resources to institutions and organizations.

Organizations are largely conservative forces in Western industrialized societies. Even as they are the repositories of great power, they often dilute and attenuate rather than focus it. Within them, power is spread among many individuals, each of whom can, alone, exercise it to only a limited extent. Even those at the top of organizational pyramids, in the governing boards, are held in check by the countervailing powers of regulatory law, judicial decisions, and some set of constituents, whether stockholders, voters, contributors, boards of directors, or customers. The separation and balance of powers are important sources of public confidence in organizations of all kinds.

Organizations are, of course, no more perfect than the people who organize and staff them. They are means through which people achieve much good and also noticeable harm. But when such harm is done, recriminations do not always begin or end with the individuals involved. Instead, blame is often directed toward the organization itself, as if it were at fault as much as or more than the individuals.

This is the source of an important question: If we know that organizational activities result from cooperation among individuals, then why attribute moral responsibility for wrongdoing to an organization instead of its human parts?

Organizations are sometimes blamed in addition to individuals. Why should this occur? Why not simply lay the problem at the feet of the individuals and leave it at that? What purpose and what justification could there be for attributing moral blame to an organization? This book seeks clear and direct answers to these questions.

My own interest in this subject arose in response to some personal experiences. The first was a tragedy I confronted as an adolescent at Millbrook School. An older student, who had kept an automatic rifle in his room, had disappeared for a few hours one evening. When all attempts to locate him had failed, school authorities sent all the students into the nearby woods to search for him. He was found dead, having committed suicide.

Although we had not known the boy well, I and my other classmates felt a strong sense of tragedy and loss. But we also felt in some ways responsible for the outcome. We pondered these matters extensively as time passed. At one point, an adult remarked that it was not us, the students, who were at fault, but the school. I wondered what that might mean and how it could be true. After all, the school was run by the very finest people with the very best of intentions for all the students.

It was indeed because of the example and impact of my teachers there that I first thought of becoming a teacher. It was in part because those teachers invited the students to question, propose, and examine answers and to discuss important issues that I wondered for years about the meaning of those tragic events. Ultimately, I wondered if a school or any organization could be to blame for anything, if its constituents were not.

My questions persisted unanswered for years, until, as an adult, I witnessed what was in some ways a similar phenomenon. This time, however, my perspective was that of an outsider. I had moved to a small city that contained a factory that had made munitions used in the Vietnam War. Some of my friends were research scientists who worked for the company. War protesters had condemned the company and its employees for their part in an immoral war.

I opposed the war, as did many of my friends. Like them, I regretted the complicity of their employer. What puzzled me was that some of my friends blamed their employer, but did not accept blame themselves. I wondered how the company could be to blame if its personnel were not. My pursuit of these and related questions led me to the subject of this book.

The ensuing analysis is based on the conviction that the blaming of organizations is an important aspect of our moral and social lives. It is important in our personal lives because we attribute some of our own misfortunes to the errant ways of organizations. We blame organizations and the ways they are allowed to function for much that is wrong with society. In our political lives, legal penalties directed at organizations are believed to be justifiable and thus legitimate in part to the extent that organizations are held blameworthy. If we tried to refrain from blaming organizations, we would have to give up responsibility and control of much that is wrong in our lives.[1] When we lack full knowledge of individual blameworthiness for what has gone wrong, we still may hold out hope for accountability and potential improvement by blaming an organization. No matter that the organization is not itself human: it is a human development, created by humans for humans, and is controlled by humans. It should and can be fully responsive to human needs. To blame it may embody beliefs that humans are not completely the pawns of fate, and have not lost control, and that improvements can be made. And if it is indefensible to blame organizations, then so much the worse for ideas of just dessert and retributive justice toward them.

None of this should be taken to imply that belief in organizational blameworthiness is absolutely indispensable in human life. The point is that this belief plays a role in individual, social, and political life, that role is far from trivial, and is not likely to be eliminated from our lives. However, such blameworthiness is often misunderstood. This study is directed to clarify the meanings and significance of attributions of organizational moral blame through a study of its purposes and the relevant evidence supporting it. The book endeavors to contribute to a clearer, richer, and more sensitive appreciation of organizational blame. It is not directed to provide ready solutions to questions of meaning, or to moral or ontological questions raised by such attributions of blame. Its purpose is not to establish that a statement blaming an organization is committed to any one meaning. Rather, one may blame an organization meaningfully without commitment to a thesis as radical at that of Peter French that the organization is in fact, ontologically speaking, a moral person. Indeed, one may intend any of several possible meanings by attributing blame to an organization.

The question, "Why blame the organization?" is, of course, ambiguous. It may mean, "What purpose is there for blaming the organization?" or "What evidence is there that the organization deserves blame?" Furthermore, it may mean, "What purpose is best served by blaming the organization?" or, "What is the best evidence to support one's blaming the organization?" The ensuing analysis unfolds from an examination of both the purposes for and the evidence available to support one's blaming of an organization.  Investigation of each main interpretation of the question illuminates some important aspects of our thinking about the blaming of organizations.  Clarification of the purposes of and evidence for such blame facilitates a more accurate assessment of it.

Two main theses emerge from investigation of the purpose of and evidence for such blame.  First is the thesis of individual sufficiency, that blaming an organization does not best fulfill the significant purposes of blaming if the fault of all individuals responsible for the blameworthy matter is fully known.  Second is the thesis of individual dependency, that there can be no good evidence to support the blaming of an organization without evidence that some of its personnel are to some extent responsible for the matter at hand.  Together, these two reveal important relationships between individual and organizational blameworthiness.  In addition, they mark limits to the relevant evidence and significant meaning of attributions of organizational blame.

Although the relationship between these two theses has not been noticed or appreciated, some of the content of the theses has been noted before.  Suggesting the sufficiency thesis, Martin Benjamin has pointed out that when we have full knowledge of all the individuals who are blameworthy for something, and full knowledge of the extent of their blameworthiness, "calling both the action and the responsibility 'collective' adds nothing substantive to the characterization of the case."[2]  Suggesting the dependency thesis, Virginia Held wrote, "This is not to say that because we cannot assign moral responsibility distributively in the case of an organized group, no one is morally responsible; for surely decision methods alone are not capable of 'acting'."[3]  Benjamin's comment has been largely ignored by writers on the subject, and Held seems to have repudiated her view in a later writing.[4]  The dependency and sufficiency theses thus require extensive defense, developed in the first three chapters.

Sufficiency and dependency form an important part of five conditions for attributing moral blame to organizations.  These are proposed in chapter two as conditions for making warranted assertions, not as conditions of truth.  Due to their formal nature, they allow that various speakers with various motives may meaningfully attribute moral responsibility to organizations for a variety of reasons.  The five conditions admit, for example, recognition of a limited value to Peter French's theory of corporate moral personhood, and to Larry May's theory of vicarious negligence.  In addition, they accommodate important pragmatic dimensions of our reasoning about the blameworthiness of organizations.

The analysis recognizes a number of purposes why people attribute blame to organizations.  One in particular has been entirely neglected and reveals an important dimension of such blame.  This purpose arises when one has limited evidence of the blameworthiness of individuals, and evidence that their blameworthiness arose in the context of and due to the influence of some organizational involvement. We may at times blame an organization precisely because of a shortage of evidence of individual blameworthiness, together with evidence that blameworthiness likely arose as a result of organizational influence. Finding fault with an organization in such circumstances may serve certain moral purposes better than a more tempered blaming of individuals, even if the latter is more firmly supported by the available evidence.

The origins, goals, and methods of the analysis are broadly pragmatic in following much of the outlook of philosophers such as Peirce, James, Dewey, and Quine. The analysis begins from a study of the practical consequences of attributing blame to organizations. It examines both the goals of blaming and the evidence available to justify it. It progresses from examining available evidence to investigating the question of what that evidence is sufficient to establish.

The analysis does not rely on or assume the truth of any allegedly fundamental moral, metaphysical, ontological, or epistemological distinctions, or what Dewey called "dualisms." Rather, the analysis is bolstered by a detailed repudiation in chapters two and five of the ontological dualism created by Peter French's distinction between aggregate and conglomerate collectivities. In the end, it is mainly by degree that the rationale for and import of blaming organizations differs from those of blaming groups and other collectivities.

The analysis does not begin from the standpoint of some thesis about the deep structure of reality. It does not begin from some metaphysical or ontological theory about the nature of organizations or other collectivities. Rather, it analyzes our thought and language by studying first the nature of claims about the blameworthiness of organizations. It begins with an inquiry into the kind of thinking which ordinarily leads one to blame an organization instead of simply the individuals who might be partly at fault. Some of the results of the investigation are captured in the five conditions for plausibly blaming an organization. These do not provide definitive, necessary and sufficient conditions for the truth of such attributions of blame. Rather, they reveal that such attributions of blame are reasonable within a certain range of evidence, and unreasonable beyond it. This range is delineated by the theses of individual sufficiency and dependency. These reveal that blaming an organization is most clearly defensible when there is a certain kind of limited evidence of individual blameworthiness present, and not too much.

The intermediate range of the evidence supporting claims of organizational blame reveals that such blame is pragmatic in nature. To attribute moral blameworthiness to an organization may be reasonable in the presence of certain kinds of evidence and certain purposes. But such blame cannot be defended by the same kind of moral basis as a claim of individual moral blameworthiness. It may make sense to blame organizations as if they are persons. But such blame is not rationally defensible on the basis of the same criteria one may use to warrant a claim that an individual is to blame. If one could formulate necessary and sufficient conditions for individual blameworthiness, the five conditions and the sufficiency and dependency theses reveal that one cannot do so for the blameworthiness of organizations. There is little justification for claiming that organizations are blameworthy, ontologically speaking, for the same kinds of reasons that one may claim that humans are. If it appears that humans may be inherently blameworthy regardless of anyone's purposes for attributing blame, the sufficiency and dependency theses and the five conditions are reasons why organizations may not. One's purposes for blaming are an inextricable part of the justification of any attribution of organizational blame.

Another pragmatic aspect of such blame is its uncertainty. I argue in chapter one that one can have too much evidence to warrant blaming an organization. If so, uncertainty is an integral part of such blame. To marshall evidence in excess of that specified by the sufficiency thesis does not establish that the organization is more surely to blame. Rather, it finesses the need to blame the organization, revealing instead that one could more appropriately blame the relevant individuals. Thus, all justifiable attributions of blame toward an organization are based on limited evidence and thus cannot be totally, irrefutably conclusive. Pragmatic concepts are useful and enlightening to a degree, but make no claim of final truth. Attributions of organizational blame are typically pragmatic in their essential uncertainty as well as their responsiveness to purposes.

Chapter one provides initial support for the sufficiency thesis by arguing that, in the presence of full knowledge of individual blameworthiness, the main, characteristic purposes of blaming are better served by blaming individuals than organizations. That is, when one has full knowledge of the individuals who are blameworthy for some event, the main purposes for attributing blame are better served by attributing it to the individuals than by attributing it to the organization. And nothing significant is gained by attributing it to the organization in addition to the individuals.

Chapter two defends the dependency thesis against the claims of Peter French, arguing that the purposes of blaming an organization are defeated by the admission that none of the personnel of the organization are in any way to blame for the matter at hand. If none of the personnel are in any way to blame, then there is no good reason to attribute blameworthiness, in its typically moral sense, to anything. The five conditions are formulated later in the chapter, and the resultant analysis is defended in chapter three against several apparently problematic cases and possible objections.

Chapter four spells out the implications of the five conditions for understanding questions of the distribution of blame within an organization and the meaning and evidence of attributions of organizational moral blame. These conditions allow considerable openness, flexibility, and pluralism in the answers to such questions pertaining to a wide variety of cases. The chapter eschews efforts to identify a single, true meaning of attributions of organizational blame.

Chapter five develops a sustained attack on the ontological basis of Peter

French's theory of corporate moral personhood. The point of the attack is to show that French's distinction between two fundamentally different kinds of collectivities is incoherent. However, this does not prove that corporations can never be viewed intelligibly as moral persons.

Chapter six shows that Larry May's analysis of collective responsibility fails to address many of the most important questions regarding the subject. It systematically ignores questions of the conditions of such attributions of blame, the referent of such attributions, their meaning, and appropriate evidence. However, May's theory of vicarious negligence, as far as it goes, is easily accommodated by the analysis developed from the five conditions.

Chapter seven addresses questions of the similarities and differences between the blameworthiness of organizations and less organized groups of people. It examines the meaning of claims that various groups are to blame and the conditions under which blame is best attributed to individuals, groups, or organizations. It reveals that such matters are best addressed in light of pragmatic considerations based on justifiable purposes. The chapter confirms a major finding of chapter five: that differences between the blameworthiness of organizations and groups are mainly differences of degree.

Chapter eight investigates questions of the justification of punishment. It argues that there is no important ontological distinction between the punishment of organizations and the punishment of less organized groups. It reveals that appropriate versions of both the sufficiency and dependency theses pertain to our considered thinking about the justification of punishment.

Chapter nine explores the relationship of the analysis to the philosophical issues surrounding methodological individualism, moral realism, and pragmatism. Although largely individualistic and antirealist in its implications, the analysis does not rule out all aspects of methodological holism or moral realism. The analysis does, of course, take a pragmatic approach, and reveals that organizational blameworthiness is best understood as a pragmatic concept. Some general aspects of pragmatic thought are identified in the final part of the chapter, and their relationship to the analysis is clarified. In the end, blaming an organization is best understood not as based on justified blameworthiness, but as an attempt to grapple morally with a body of information characterized by uncertainty about the moral blameworthiness of individual humans. Finally, the analysis does not offer easy answers or recommend radical revision of responsible, ordinary thinking about the blameworthiness of organizations. Rather, it counsels those who would blame organizations to examine, with a critical eye, both their purposes and the evidence supporting them.

**Notes**

1. This view is in marked contrast to the early views of Professors Sidney Hook and Hywel Lewis, who maintain a kind of radical individualistic reductionism to the effect that claims of collective blame are atavistic simplifications that can be best clarified by reduction to some combination of the blameworthiness of individuals. Joseph Epstein, "Remembering Sidney Hook," *Commentary* 88, no. 5 (1989): 41-47; H. D. Lewis, "Collective Responsibility," in *Collective Responsibility: Five Decades of Debate in Theoretical and Applied Ethics,* ed. Larry May and Stacey Hoffman (Savage, MD: Rowman and Littlefield, 1991), 23-26.

2. Martin Benjamin, "Can Moral Responsibility Be Collective and Nondistributive?," *Social Theory and Practice* 4 (1976): 94.

3. Virginia Held, "Moral Responsibility and Collective Action," in *Individual and Collective Responsibility: The Massacre at My Lai,* ed. Peter A. French (Cambridge, MA: Schenkman, 1972), 115.

4. Virginia Held, "Corporations, Persons, and Responsibility," in *Shame, Responsibility and the Corporation,* ed. Hugh Curtler (New York: Haven, 1986), 162.

# Acknowledgments

The idea for this book first developed at a summer seminar sponsored by the National Endowment for the Humanities in 1987 in San Antonio, Texas. The director of the seminar, Professor Peter French, spared the members of the seminar none of his energy, always willing to read and discuss whatever we gave him. He challenged my thinking at a very high level. That hot summer was a time of great productivity for all twelve members of the seminar, who created an atmosphere that brought out the best in all of us. Judith Andre and David Risser were of special help to my own thinking on the subject of this book.

Delta College supported most of the initial writing of the manuscript by providing a sabbatical in 1992, spent at the University of Oxford, England. Rev. David Atkinson, Chaplain of Corpus Christi College, helped me establish a connection with the college and helped me open communication with Professor Bernard Williams, who read the most central parts of the manuscript as it emerged. Much of the clarity of the argument in the first three chapters resulted from responses to his insightful and stringent criticisms. Several of the topics in chapter three, including the "sea of green fallacy" were largely suggested by my discussions with him.

Some of my first careful thinking on the subject appeared in "The Responsibility of Men for the Oppression of Women," *Journal of Applied Philosophy* 2 (1985): 217-29. I presented a paper to the Western Division of the American Philosophical Association in Chicago in 1985 entitled, "Individual and Collective Responsibility and Punishment." In that paper, I began to work through ideas about the dependency thesis and the relationship of the justification of punishment to a variety of different kinds of attributions of collective moral responsibility. These ideas were developed further in "The

Meaning and Justification of Collective Moral Responsibility," *Public Affairs Quarterly* 2, no. 3 (1988): 69-83, which explores ideas about distributivity and reductionism, which form a central part of the analysis in chapter four. Finally, Kluwer Academic Publishers gave me permission to use, as the main part of chapter five, "The Central Distinction in the Theory of Corporate Moral Personhood," *Journal of Business Ethics* 9 (1990): 473-80.

My colleague, Professor Ralph Forsberg of Delta College, deserves special thanks for taking the time to read and critique the manuscript, suggesting many changes, and helping me to understand better how it may be read and interpreted. Professor Carl Wellman of Washington University read several parts of the manuscript, and offered some important suggestions. Chester Mahaffey, professor emeritus of Northwood University, contributed to the final draft by his numerous suggestions for improving its writing style.

Fritz Hemker of Kenyon College gave me some helpful tips on the use of Wordperfect 5.1 at a crucial point. I owe special gratitude to Johanna Frohm of Delta College, who gave generously of her time, helping lead me past some enormous frustration and exasperation in formatting the manuscript.

Finally, Deirdre Mullervy, the production editor at Rowman and Littlefield, contributed to my effort by her patience and tolerance.

# Chapter 1

## Purposes of Attributing Moral Blame

Attributing moral blame to organizations is common in contemporary life. Why people do so and the reasons to think it is appropriate or plausible in various situations are the central questions addressed in this study. It is an inquiry into the purposes, justification, and meaning of this blame. It assumes that such attributions have a certain intuitive significance. That is, a thoughtful member of our culture could, with some effort, clarify some of their implications. Further, one could produce considerations to support or dispute them. However, there are important questions about such attributions that are not immediately clear.

Consider, first, the question of what sense it could make to blame an organization. We blame people for failing to control their pets and we also appear to blame dogs for fouling the sidewalk. But there is an important difference here. We appear to blame the dogs because they caused the messes, but we blame their owners because they could and should have curbed their dogs. We blame the owners in a full, moral sense, but we blame the dogs in a nonmoral sense.[1] Which sense of blame is at stake when one blames the organization?

The answer is that either sense might be intended by one blaming an organization. One might mean that the organization caused a problem or that it is morally to blame for the problem. The attribution of nonmoral blame is not particularly troublesome, for there are many understandable ways in which an organization might be said to have caused something to happen. But the moral sense of blame, when attributed to an organization, raises further questions.

Human beings can be blameworthy if they are intelligent, have the ability to choose in a deliberate, rational way, and have certain moral duties. However, it may appear that such things can be said of organizations only in elliptical ways. Of course there are some ways in which organizations are similar to human beings. But there are others in which they differ. Can one blame an organization in the same moral sense that one blames a person? Just what evidence is there to support an assertion that an organization is to blame? Why would one want to level moral blame at an organization instead of its personnel? These are central questions to be investigated below.

The present chapter is directed to clarify people's purposes in leveling moral blame at an organization. It proceeds by addressing, first, the nature of moral blame as it is attributed to individuals. Second, the blaming of organizations is distinguished from the blaming of groups, and questions unique to the former are set forth. Section three begins the inquiry into the purposes for blaming groups by describing a procedure one might follow to determine if one or more individuals are to blame. Section four investigates the reasons why it may be unsatisfying to restrict one's blame to individuals. The next section argues that if the blameworthiness of all people who are blameworthy for something is known, there is no significant moral reason to blame, in addition, an organization. Finally, section six offers an enumeration and initial clarification of the purposes for blaming an organization.

## 1.1 Blame and Responsibility

We level blame in the moral sense when something has gone wrong and we are offended by some untoward action, act of omission, ongoing practice, intent, belief, feeling, or state of affairs. To attribute blame is to assert that some party or parties is morally responsible for some untoward matter, and deserves to be held accountable, or responsible. Indeed, attributing blame may itself be a means of holding one accountable.

The act of holding someone morally responsible is different from the state of being morally responsible. One may be morally responsible for something even though one is never in fact held responsible for it by anyone. But if one is to be held responsible for some untoward act, there are many ways of doing so. One might be brought before the law, brought face to face with a person one has wronged, punished, or simply told, "You are being held responsible." To hold someone responsible usually involves blame, at least implicitly. And in order to be blamed justifiably, the person must be morally responsible and blameworthy.

Under what conditions could one say that a person is morally responsible for something? A definitive statement of such conditions is not easy to provide. Many discussions of the subject indicate that an individual must (a) be causally responsible, (b) have intended to act accordingly, and (c) have been able to do otherwise. As reasonable as they sound at first, problems arise for each of these criteria, and extensive debates have ensued.

People are often held responsible for their acts of omission, although an act of omission is not obviously something one causes to occur.[2] However, some philosophers have argued that there is an important sense in which one can reasonably be said to be causally responsible for acts of omission.[3] Some have objected to the second requirement on the grounds that people are in fact sometimes held responsible for actions and results they did not intend. Extensive debate has ensued over the question of just what the relevant intention may be.[4] Some have argued that the intentionality requirement can be replaced by merely requiring that one could have foreseen what consequences may have resulted.[5] Henry Tam has argued on Aristotelian grounds that moral responsibility can be accounted for in terms of personal qualities and awareness of one's own behavior.[6] Regarding the third requirement, just what it means to be able to do otherwise has been challenged and debated at length, as has the question of whether this should be a requirement at all.[7]

The main theses of this book do not turn on any one fully complete and adequate analysis of the requirements of moral responsibility. These theses could be stated in ways consistent with a number of different formulations of the conditions for and meaning of claims of moral responsibility. However, thorough treatment of the issues addressed below requires reference to some set of conditions under which moral responsibility is warranted. The formulation offered here is suggested merely as a touchstone for the ensuing analysis rather than as a definitive statement.

Because the present concern is with blaming, questions of moral responsibility in contexts of praise are largely ignored. However, development of an acceptable analysis and understanding of blaming would clear the way for a corresponding and derivative analysis and understanding of moral responsibility in contexts of praise. Study of moral responsibility for wrongdoing is in many respects the more challenging and interesting task, and the one which has received the lion's share of attention. In light of the work done by others on the subject, the following three may serve as a tentative list of conditions that are each individually necessary and, taken together, sufficient to identify a case in which one or more persons are morally responsible for some wrong, and thus worthy of blame.

(a)     Something untoward occurred, and it likely would have been prevented by one or more persons taking appropriate measures that were not taken.

(b)     There was a moral duty for those people to take those measures.

(c)    They could have taken the measures and have no good moral excuse for not having done so.

To determine that such conditions are fulfilled, one need not address them in exactly the order they are presented here.

Fulfillment of the three requirements involves considerable judgment. Whether a given untoward occurrence is sufficiently objectionable to warrant moral blame is a matter which may be far from clear. The occurrence itself may border on the trivial. One may be situated so remotely from the occurrence as to deserve no significant degree of blame for it.[8]

Whether or not the measures in question, or any measures, for that matter, likely would have prevented the untoward occurrence may, in practice, be difficult to ascertain. It may be unclear, for example, whether a certain level of alcohol in one's blood was a sufficient cause of an automobile accident. There may be no way to determine conclusively whether the person would have avoided the accident successfully if one had a lower level of blood alcohol.

Furthermore, it may be difficult to determine whether or not one did or did not take appropriate measures to prevent the untoward result. One might have taken some of those measures but not others. Or one may have taken some such measures to an inadequate extent.

Whether or not there was a moral duty for one to take those measures may depend upon differing points of view about people's responsibilities in the situation. What counts as a good moral excuse may also be controversial.

These and other such questions may give rise to borderline cases creating difficulties in the effort to arrive at a justified basis for attributing blame. That there are such cases is undeniable and sometimes important in real day-to-day efforts to attribute blame. However, they do not prove, in the eyes of most, at least, that the very concept of justified blame is spurious. There are, in fact, cases that fit the criteria quite clearly. Despite the existence of such borderline cases, people do in fact apply criteria of similar kinds in ordinary, day-to-day efforts to determine whether blame is appropriate.

It is important to note that these requirements allow the possibility that one person may be more to blame than another and the possibility of several sharing blame for some misdeed.[9] They allow the possibility that blame may be attributed to groups of people and also to organizations. Clarification of such attributions and their purposes emerge as the discussion proceeds.

The ensuing analysis proceeds from consideration of individual blame to examination of blame directed at organizations. In doing this, no assumption is made that blame directed at individuals is metaphysically or epistemologically prior to or more fundamental than blame directed at groups or organizations. But we seem to have better established knowledge about individual blame. This knowledge can help clarify the similarities and differences among the three.

## 1.2 Blaming Groups and Organizations

When the negligence of several individuals results in some untoward effect, one may be inclined to name the group of individuals as blameworthy instead of naming each separately. One might say, after a football game, "The Lions fans in this part of the stadium are to blame for the mess." Apart from the question of how many of them are to blame, such a statement is not particularly puzzling, whether or not it is true. The question of whether one is referring to some or all of the fans in this part of the stadium can easily be clarified by asking the speaker what one means.

Consider three main senses in which the statement is clear: (1) It is clear to whom blame is being attributed: all or some of the members of a particular group of Lions fans. (2) It is clear what evidence would be needed to establish the likely truth of the statement: evidence that all or some of the members of this group of fans deserves some blame for the mess. (3) The motives of one making such a statement can be identified by asking that person or by observing the circumstances surrounding the utterance of the statement. The person might have made the statement out of disgust, frustration, moral indignation, or in order to direct the police. Such a statement is ordinarily a shorthand way of attributing a share of moral blame to a number of individuals without naming them individually.

The same kind of clarity would not obtain, however, for a statement blaming the architectural firm that designed the stadium for the collapse of a section of it during a football game. (1) It is not clear to whom the blame is being attributed. The speaker may be directing blame at neither all nor some particular personnel in the firm. If asked, the speaker might admit that some of the personnel in the firm are surely not to blame, such as some of the secretaries and the president's chauffeur. Yet, the speaker may insist that some architects in the firm should have known that under certain conditions, there could be a collapse.

If some architects did know this, perhaps they are to blame. But then why is the firm to blame? Just what is being blamed if not the individual architects in the firm? And if some secretaries do not deserve blame, but the firm does, are the secretaries not in the firm? Just what is the firm? Could the secretaries be to blame just because they happen to be in this firm? Could the firm be to blame but not all of its personnel? Some who make such a claim may be unsure of that to which they are referring and unclear on the question of which possible meaning of the statement is best supported by the evidence and which best fulfills the most defensible purposes at hand.

(2) It is not clear what evidence would be needed to establish the truth of the statement that the firm is to blame. Regardless of questions of the precise make-up of the architectural firm, our speaker might well be willing to distinguish the firm from its personnel. That is, the speaker might grant that

some of its personnel are not to blame for the collapse. Yet, at the same time, the speaker might believe that the responsibility of certain key personnel in the firm can warrant the claim that the firm is responsible. But how can this be? How can the fact that some members of the firm have a certain characteristic support a claim that the characteristic is true of the whole firm as well?

Suppose, on the other hand, that everyone in the firm was at fault, and was proved to have been involved in a large scheme of fraud. It is not at all clear that this warrants the claim that the firm itself as a unitary entity is to blame. If one thinks of the firm as nothing more than the collection of all its personnel, then, of course, it would be to blame. But it may seem that the firm is something more than just a group of people. If so, then just what in addition to the blameworthiness of the individuals in it is needed to justify the claim that the firm is to blame?

(3) Finally, there is a special problem of purposes or motives regarding blame leveled at the architectural firm. Of course, the purpose of leveling blame might be to vent frustration or to encourage one to pursue a lawsuit. But it is not at all clear why one would blame the firm as a unity instead of qualifying one's statement and blaming, say, just the architects who designed the stadium. That people blame organizations in such a way is clear. That they sometimes do so in earnest is also clear. What is achieved by doing so apart from vindictiveness, convenience, or careless talk is far from clear. These questions are pursued in the remainder of this first chapter.

## 1.3 From Blaming Individuals to Blaming Organizations

If the blaming of individuals is intuitively clearer and better understood than the blaming of organizations, then the question arises as to why one would even bother to blame an organization. Indeed, it is revealing to consider the kinds of circumstances and purposes which motivate one to move from blaming individual people to blaming organizations. A grasp of these may help clarify the kinds of evidence which justify blaming organizations and the meaning of statements attributing such blame. To understand why people make this move, consider first the purpose of blaming individuals, and the reasoning one uses to establish the plausibility of such blame.

The search for someone to blame is usually set off by the discovery that something unfortunate, harmful or in some way untoward has occurred. Consider the grounding of the supertanker, *Exxon Valdez*, in Prince William Sound, Alaska, at 12:04 AM on March 24th, 1989.[10] Once the untoward event is identified, one might, first, cast about to discover whether someone could have prevented it. If nature alone caused the occurrence and no human beings could have prevented the grounding, the search for an object of blame may cease.

If, on the other hand, humans might have prevented it, one may then proceed to determine the measures which might have been taken to prevent the massive spill. In this case, investigators of the National Transportation Safety Board discovered that Captain Hazelwood had been drinking heavily just prior to departure, was not at the helm as the ship was leaving the Sound, and that a series of other infractions of maritime rules had occurred.[11] Because he was competent when sober, and had made the trip before, it is reasonable to think that his sober, attentive presence on the bridge likely would have led to avoidance of the error in navigation.

Second, one must determine whether or not there was, pertaining to the case, a relevant moral duty that should have been fulfilled, but was not. One determines what the duty was, who had it, and whether or not any people in the situation violated that duty. It may appear, in the case at hand, that there was a moral duty of tanker captains to exercise their responsibilities. It may appear that sobriety is necessary to do so, and that the captain did not fulfill these and other duties appropriately.[12]

Third, one determines whether or not the captain has any significant exculpatory excuses. Suppose one determines that he does not, and was inexcusably lax and irresponsible given the magnitude of his responsibilities. As a result, one may judge him as morally responsible, at least in part, for the disaster, and thus deserving of some blame for it.[13]

There may, of course, be other individuals beside the captain who also deserve blame for the disaster. However, whether or not there are may well be irrelevant to the question of whether the captain himself is to blame. If the three conditions are clearly met regarding the captain, then he is blameworthy to that extent.

## 1.4 When Is Individual Responsibility Not Enough?

The initial circumstances that lead one to consider blaming an organization are no different from those above. Something untoward occurs. The *Exxon Valdez* hit bottom twice, resulting in a massive oil spill. One's dismay with the outcome suggests the question of whether the event could and should have been prevented by human beings. Perhaps they should have taken measures they did not in fact take. Assuming that it is clear that the captain could and should have taken those measures and has no exculpatory excuse for not doing so, then he is to blame for the spill.

There may be important reasons not to conclude the inquiry regarding the grounding with the blameworthiness of the captain. It seems possible that others also deserve some moral blame. The third mate, who took control after the pilot had left the ship and the captain had left the bridge, might well have performed his duties carelessly. The managers in charge of the shipping division at Exxon might have taken more care to follow up on Captain Hazelwood's subsequent response to treatment for alcoholism in 1985.[14] The

U.S. Coast Guard might have taken steps to ensure that Exxon and other ship owners were enforcing both federal and company regulations regarding alcohol and drugs on board ships, and consumption prior to embarking.[15]   Any number of people may deserve significant blame for the crash.

At this point in the inquiry, we have identified (a) one likely blameworthy person, (b) another possibly blameworthy individual, and (c) the possibility of an indefinite number of other blameworthy individuals.   There is now a direction for further inquiry and two different hypotheses to investigate in order to clarify the full extent of the blame for the grounding.   But there is not, as yet, any clear reason to blame an organization instead of individuals.

Suppose that further inquiry had produced evidence that memos on the need to enforce alcohol and drug use on board ship had circulated in the shipping division at Exxon two years earlier.   Suppose that a few brief discussions had taken place, but that the questions had been largely set aside.   And suppose that one manager had found a memo issued ten years earlier by an Exxon vice president stating that enforcement of maritime regulations was the job of the Coast Guard, not the company.   Suppose, finally, once informed of this viewpoint, subordinates in the company, who are now known and identified, and who did not agree with this influential manager, had dropped the issue.

The point here is to consider a fully known, complex set of events within the corporation that led to a deliberate failure to enforce certain regulations regarding personnel aboard Exxon's ships.   Why, in such a case, might one be inclined to blame the Exxon organization instead of the known individuals?   If the course of events leading to the deliberate lack of enforcement is fully known and described by reference to individuals, their moral and professional duties, their actions, practices, failings, roles, and interrelations through the organization, then why even consider blaming, in addition to or instead of these individuals, the organization itself?   Why blame the organization if the full moral responsibility of all the blameworthy individuals is, in fact, fully understood?   That is, if we know all the individual humans who are blameworthy for a given matter, we know all the various reasons each is to blame, we know the extent to which each is to blame, and we know that no other humans are to blame, then why consider blaming the organization?

This question does not ask if there is any evidence to support a charge that the organization is blameworthy in such circumstances.   Rather, it asks if we need to make such a charge.   It asks if there is any significant purpose served by making the charge and trying to substantiate it.   If there is such a purpose, then clarifying it should help illuminate the meaning of the charge and the sorts of evidence that might best confirm or disconfirm it.   If, on the other hand, there is no such purpose, then an important limitation of the charge will be clear.   Pursuit of this question occupies the next section, producing the view that there is unlikely to be a significant purpose for blaming an organization in such circumstances.

## 1.5 The Thesis of Individual Sufficiency

There are certainly many possible purposes why one might seek to blame an organization in such circumstances. However, six broad purposes can be stated that likely include the most important ones. And if we have full knowledge of the degree of blameworthiness of all the blameworthy individuals, all of these purposes can be better fulfilled by directing blame at these individuals and addressing them appropriately.

One of the most common purposes of blaming is to justify retributive punishment. If we know all the individuals who are blameworthy, and the blame is sufficient to warrant punishment, we may proceed to punish them individually, according to the level of punishment each deserves. But in attending only to the individuals, one may argue, we may have missed something. We may have missed the fact that the organization itself, quite independently of the individuals, deserves to be punished. Such a view is suggested by the work of Peter French, discussed in chapters two and five. One might argue accordingly that a corporation may deserve punishment to the extent that it is morally blameworthy. So an important purpose of blaming an organization may be to contribute to the case that it deserves punishment.

There is, however, reason to think that such a purpose is not worthwhile. If we know the degree of blameworthiness of all the individuals who are responsible for the matter at hand, we may then seek to determine whether this blameworthiness is sufficient to justify retribution against them. If it is, we may then formulate such retribution as appropriate to each individual case.

If, however, we determine that the organization is to blame, and determine that it deserves punishment on retributive grounds, we may then punish the organization as appropriate. However, here arises a significant problem. For any such measures will affect individual personnel in the organization.

Such measures will have two important disadvantages. First, some individuals who deserve no blame for the matter at hand may suffer greatly from the retributive measures directed against the organization. A fine may cause the organization to lay off workers, causing significant harm to lower-level employees who had no responsibility for the organization's misconduct. Second, some of the most blameworthy parties in the organization may escape significant inconvenience, losing neither pay nor their jobs. Punishment directed at an organization as a single entity has uneven, complex effects on its various personnel. By treating the organization in this way, as French favors, significant harm may come to some innocents, while some errant parties suffer none of the punitive effects they deserve. In its failure to treat equals equally, such an approach violates the demands of justice.

In the presence of full knowledge of individual fault, it is possible to develop punitive means that address exactly the individuals who deserve punishment and to exactly the level at which each deserves it. Such means can fulfill the demands of justice better than the crude penalties leveled against organizations.

A second possible purpose of blaming an organization, when the full blameworthiness of all the blameworthy individuals is known, might be to help direct a penalty motivated by the desire to deter in the future. The problem here is that one need not blame in order to deter. Indeed, blame is neither a necessary nor a sufficient condition to justify deterrent measures. Government agencies, for example, may have standard fines for certain infractions of their rules for purely deterrent purposes. And one's being fined for an infraction does not necessarily give any reason to think that one has done something morally wrong or deserves moral blame. So the goal or purpose of deterring either people or organizations is not a significant reason to attribute moral blame to either people or organizations, whether or not the blameworthiness of all blameworthy individuals is known.

A third purpose of blaming an organization, in the presence of full knowledge of individual blameworthiness, might be to justify a verdict of procedural justice. Perhaps a trial and its outcome in accord with legal precedent result in a certain penalty levied against an organization. Such penalty may be further justified by an attribution of organizational moral fault. However, the prospect of such justification is not likely to offer good reason to level moral blame at an organization in addition to individuals.

If we know all the individuals who are blameworthy, and an organization has broken the law, why blame the organization in order to justify penalties against it? If the organization is guilty of breaking the law, and it is judged as such, then it might be fined on grounds of strict liability.[16] Why, then, blame it morally? Should it be penalized more because it is, in addition, morally to blame? If all the blameworthy individuals are known, and their blameworthiness is known, then they can be blamed and penalized appropriately in addition to the fine required by law on grounds of strict liability. If, on the other hand, we penalize the organization more, instead of addressing the individuals, we will likely increase the injustice of the penal effects by causing some innocents to suffer and failing to give all the guilty individuals their due.[17] It is unlikely that justice is promoted in such a situation by blaming the organization either in addition to or instead of the blameworthy individuals.

A fourth possible purpose for blaming an organization in addition to all the blameworthy individuals might be to satisfy the desire to blame. According to a popular ethical tradition, wrongdoers deserve blame, regardless of whether they deserve punishment. Such a purpose is not, however, very helpful. One can, after all, blame all the blameworthy individuals just as easily as the organization itself. One can list their names and blame them appropriately. There are, moreover, some disadvantages to blaming an organization instead of its constituent individuals. Just as punishing the organization may harm innocent individuals, so blaming it indiscriminately may taint individual personnel within the organization who are entirely blameless.

A fifth answer may be that blaming an organization serves the moral purpose of laying blame where blame is due. That is, if the organization fulfills the criteria of blameworthiness enumerated in 1.1, then it is in fact blameworthy and deserves to be blamed accordingly. In that case, to blame merely the individual humans would appear to ignore a rather major source of blame: the organization itself. Despite the initial appeal of this answer, it is profoundly obfuscatory.

The question at hand is not whether an organization fits the criteria of moral blame. Rather, the question is whether any significant purpose could be served by blaming an organization if the blameworthiness of all blameworthy individuals is known. To answer this question by showing that the organization fulfills the criteria for moral blame is to assert that the purpose of blaming is to say something for which we have conclusive evidence. Such an answer denies the distinction between the purpose of a statement and its supporting evidence. Yet that is precisely the distinction upon which the present question is based. The question at hand is whether or not there is any significant purpose to blame an organization if one knows the degree of blameworthiness of all the blameworthy individuals, regardless of whether or not one has evidence that an organization fits the criteria for blameworthiness. To collapse the distinction between purpose and truth is to deny the question without providing any clear reason to do so.

A sixth possible answer to the question at hand is a variation on the fifth. This is the claim that we simply do not need to have any purpose in order to claim that an organization is blameworthy. If the claim fits the criteria for blame and is supported by significant evidence, it is true, and that is the end of the matter. We do not need any purpose to assert the statement meaningfully. Such a line of argument is, on one level, plainly gratuitous. If a statement has no identifiable, significant human purpose, to state it is to engage in a trivial act. Truth alone does not establish significance.

There is, however, another interpretation of the term "meaningful" that lends initial plausibility to the claim. This is the idea of linguistic meaning. It is true that a statement may make sense, have meaning, and thus be understandable even though there is no significant purpose in making the statement. In this sense, it may be meaningful for one to state that the organization is to blame, regardless of whether one has a significant purpose for doing so.

Such a construal of the word "meaningful" is, however, irrelevant to the question at hand. The linguistic meaningfulness of claims of organizational blame is not at issue. The question is whether there is any significant purpose served in making such claims which cannot be served as well or better by blaming individuals, when the blameworthiness of all the blameworthy individuals is known. To answer that we do not need any purpose because such blame may be meaningful is to deny without reason the distinction between the meaningfulness of a statement and the purposes it may serve.

What motivated the search here was the question of why one might consider blaming an organization such as Exxon for a disaster such as the grounding of the *Exxon Valdez* in the Prince William Sound. If sufficient evidence of individual wrongdoing appeared, it might be possible to identify all the blameworthy individuals and clarify the degree of blameworthiness of each.[18] If it is, then there is apparently no significant reason to consider leveling moral blame at some organization such as Exxon. Indeed, there are some significant disadvantages to doing so. As H. D. Lewis, Hannah Arendt, and Candace Hetzner have noted, directing blame at an organization may well have the unfortunate effect of allowing some blameworthy humans to hide behind the veil of organizational blameworthiness.[19] And as noted above, blaming an organization may cast a shadow of blameworthiness over those who do not deserve it and even encourage punitive measures against the organization, thus promoting further injustice.

None of this should be taken, however, to demonstrate that organizations should never, under any circumstances, be blamed or punished. The point is rather that full knowledge of individual blameworthiness is the point at which blame is better attributed to individuals than to organizations. This conclusion may be described as the thesis of individual sufficiency. It is the view that full knowledge of individual blame for some matter answers all significant questions of blame regarding that matter. This thesis is addressed and supported in the analysis of further examples as the discussion progresses. Sufficiency has important implications for understanding the relationship between individual and organizational blame.

If one fulfills all significant purposes of blaming by identifying all the blameworthy individuals and blaming them individually, then if blaming an organization is significant at all, it must be significant in some other set of circumstances. Specifically, it can be significant only in cases where some of the blame of some of the likely blameworthy individuals is not established. Given the sufficiency thesis, the significance of attributing organizational blame must lie in the nature of these cases. It is through examination of them that an analysis of blaming organizations is developed in the next chapter and defended beyond.

## 1.6 Purposes of Blaming an Organization

Although blaming individuals may be preferable when all individual blameworthiness is known, rarely do we have such full knowledge. In situations of lesser knowledge, significant purposes may be served by seeking to establish the blameworthiness of an organization. An appreciation of the nature and variety of such purposes is important background for the subsequent discussion.

One purpose for blaming an organization is emotional in nature, including ideas surrounding the old adage, "Misery loves company." One who is accused of wrongdoing may be comforted by the thought that in addition to oneself, some big organization is to blame. "If the organization is to blame," one may think, "then perhaps I am not so bad after all. I should not be expected to have more will-power than an entire organization." To whatever degree it may be justifiable, one's basic purpose here is to attenuate one's feeling of guilt.

A second set of purposes for blaming an organization may be to diffuse the blame that others direct at oneself. This approach may be based on the view that there is a constant amount of blame to go around. If a few people are to blame for something, it may appear as if all the blame is heaped on them. But if one can demonstrate that something as large as an organization deserves blame as well, then it may appear that less blame is available to be heaped on the individuals.[20] Something very similar to this approach is evident in the defense strategies of lawyers for some of the Nazis at the Nuremburg Trials, later in the case of Lieutenant William Calley for the massacre at My Lai, and again in the case of Oliver North for the Iran-Contra affair. If these defendants could show that an organization is to blame, others might be less inclined to seek out a few unfortunate souls to victimize and use as scapegoats.

Third, one may blame an organization as part of the justification for penalizing it. If a corporation is to blame for some harm, then fines leveled against it will be more readily accepted by its management and by the public. A trial may produce evidence which supports a guilty verdict on technical, legal grounds, but also justifies charges of moral blameworthiness. In such a case, whatever penalty is exacted may be viewed as politically and morally just. Such an outcome reinforces faith in the institutions of society.

Fourth, an organization may be blamed in order to justify compensating a victim. Perhaps no individuals have the resources to compensate some victim or set of victims to an appropriate level, but a corporation does. In that case, the corporation can be assigned most persuasively to compensate the victim if it is judged to be morally blameworthy for the initial harm.

Fifth, blaming an organization may serve to justify the revising of certain flawed policies. That is, if the organization is really to blame for some set of events, this alone is reason to make changes in organizational policies, or to change social policies and thereby lead to changes in organizational practices. Blame may thus serve as part of a strategy to influence a future course of events.

Sixth, one may blame an organization in order to justify retributive punishment toward it. One may believe that what the organization did was wrong and it simply deserves to pay for that reason and no other.

A seventh purpose of blaming an organization is to shame it. Peter French has defended the theory that shame can be an effective means of addressing and calling public attention to corporate wrongs and has advantages over various financial penalties directed toward the corporation or its personnel, whether managers or directors.[21]

The first five purposes above differ from the last two in an important respect. Blaming the organization in order to justify or achieve these first five does not play an essential role in our moral life. That is, blaming in these cases is neither a necessary nor a sufficient condition for accomplishing or justifying the main ends at hand. One can accomplish or justify those ends without blaming an organization, although establishing blameworthiness may, to be sure, enhance those other purposes to varying degrees.

The first purpose of blaming an organization, to feel less guilt and stronger self-esteem, is an emotional need that can be satisfied by means other than blaming an organization. For example, the belief that one was a victim of circumstances can suffice. The conviction that one is basically a good person, despite a mistake, can also help one to overcome feelings of guilt.

The second purpose is to reduce the blame that others direct at oneself. In these cases, one seeks to convince others that one deserves a lesser degree of blame than might at first appear. Again, such a purpose can be achieved in many different ways. One can prove to others that one really was a victim of circumstances or that one acted out of good motives. Or one may demonstrate to them that one is, in all other respects, a good person.

The third purpose, that of justifying penalties against an organization, can also be achieved without blaming the organization. One can justify penalties on utilitarian grounds, arguing that it is best for society that the organization be penalized. Or one can justify penalties on the grounds that they are warranted by the law, the rules of society, which the organization is bound to follow. Strict liability can be used as a plausible basis for some penalties.

The fourth purpose of blaming an organization is that of enhancing the case that an organization should compensate a victim. There may be many good reasons apart from blameworthiness why it is appropriate for the organization to make reparations. Perhaps such practice is required by the law or is best for society in any number of different respects. As with the first three purposes, attributions of blame to an organization are not essential to achieving this one, although they may aid in the effort to justify it.

The fifth purpose, of justifying changes in policy in order to influence future organizational practice, does not require blaming. If the policies have, do or will cause harm, violate laws or cause people to commit immoral or questionable acts, these may be sufficient reasons to change the policies. It is doubtful that adding an attribution of blame adds anything to the argument that the policies need changing. Indeed, an attribution of blame itself presupposes that the organizational practice is somehow is wrong, unlawful or harmful. If so, then the practice should have been and should be different. Of course this may serve as partial justification for blaming the organization. But blaming it does not add something new to the case for making changes in policy.

Attributing moral blameworthiness to an organization is, however, essential to achieving the sixth and seventh purposes described above. Neither retribution nor shame can be justified unless the object of it is indeed worthy of blame. Retribution is addressed in more depth in chapter eight, which considers the relevance of organizational blameworthiness to punishment.

Shame is a means of holding one responsible by calling attention to one's blameworthiness. We shame someone because we believe that person is blameworthy and, in addition, deserves the discomfort of being recognized by others as blameworthy. Shame is thus, in part, a mild form of retributive punishment. The treatment of punishment in chapter eight thus applies, *mutatis mutandis* to considerations of shame.

Before concluding the initial treatment of the purposes of blaming an organization, it is important to consider an eighth purpose that differs from the first seven in a number of ways. This arises when no plausible combination of blame laid upon individuals is sufficient to account for the case at hand. There are situations in which there is evidence indicating that blame is deserved on a large scale. However, efforts to identify the blameworthy individuals meet with only limited success. In such cases, one may seek to level blame in a way that would likely capture all the probable blameworthy individuals and at the same time account for the milieu through which this blameworthiness accrued. That is, one attributes blame in a speculative way, exceeding the evidence available. Lacking firm evidence of all the people who deserve blame for some matter, but having evidence that the likely ones are connected through some organization and evidence that the organizational connections are an important factor in their blameworthiness, one jumps the gap and blames the organization. One may blame the organization, then, in order to blame something when there is limited evidence of blameworthy individuals, but it is likely that organizational ties among them are an important source of their blameworthiness.

This eighth purpose of blaming an organization is particularly relevant in light of the thesis of individual sufficiency. According to that thesis, there is no significant purpose served by blaming an organization for something in the presence of a complete account of all the individuals who are blameworthy for it. According to the eighth purpose, one reason to blame an organization is precisely because such a complete account is lacking.

The eighth purpose may appear, at first, somewhat obscure, and not likely to be cited as a purpose by those who blame organizations. However, it is far more important than first appears. Its nature and importance are clarified further in the following chapters.

## 1.7 Chapter Summary

Beginning with the fact that people do at times blame organizations, some of the significance of this was noted in a general way, which raised the question of how blame is related to moral responsibility. Three criteria for determining a case of moral blame were enumerated, and the blaming of groups was compared to the blaming of organizations. It was noted that in comparison to blaming individuals and groups of people, blaming organizations is unclear or problematic in several respects. That clarity can best be developed from the standpoint of this firmer grasp of the moral blameworthiness of individuals.

What first motivates blame of either individuals or organizations is some untoward event, process, or practice. Consideration of an ecological disaster led to a description of the circumstances and reasoning under which one attributes blame to individuals. Next, the question of when and why one might need to attribute blame to an organization instead of simply to all the blameworthy individuals was raised and examined. This led to the question of whether there might be any significant purpose to blame an organization in conditions of complete knowledge of individual blameworthiness, where one knows fully the degree of blame properly attributed to all the individuals who were responsible for the disaster. Examination of all the likely purposes produced no compelling purpose for doing so. Indeed, each of the significant purposes of blaming could be achieved as well or better, in such circumstances, by addressing the blameworthiness of individuals, and avoiding the blameworthiness of an organization. This is part of the thesis of individual sufficiency--that organizations are significantly blamed only if there is a significant degree of incompleteness in our understanding of the individual blame for some untoward matter.

Finally, seven typical purposes for blaming organizations were enumerated and clarified. Of these, it is mainly the purposes of justifying retributive punishment and shaming that play an important role in our moral life. An eighth purpose was then cited, although it has rarely been clearly indicated by those seeking to lay blame. It is a purpose that might arise in the presence of an incomplete grasp of individual blame. This is the purpose of attributing blame to an organization when established individual blame is insufficient to account for all the blame which is likely deserved. It is a purpose that emerges more clearly from the analysis of evidence for organizational blame to be developed in the next chapter.

## Notes

1. *cf.* Kurt Baier, "Guilt and Responsibility," in *Individual and Collective Responsibility,* ed. French, 51-52; Kurt Baier, "Moral and Legal Responsibility," in *Medical Innovation and Bad Outcomes: Legal, Social and Ethical Responses,*

ed. Mark Siegler, Stephen Toulmin, Franklin Zimring, Kenneth Schaffner (Ann Arbor: Health Administration, 1987), 102-111.

2. *cf.* H. L. A. Hart and Tony Honore, *Causation in the Law*, 2nd ed. (Oxford: Oxford University, 1985), 38, 50-51, 59, 127-128, 411-418, 447-9.

3. Elazar Weinryb, "Omissions and Responsibility," *Philosophical Quarterly* 30 (1980): 1-18; John C. Hall, "Acts and Omissions," *Philosophical Quarterly* 39 (1989): 399-408.

4. Gilbert Harman, "Practical Reasoning," *Review of Metaphysics* 29 (1976): 431-463; Arthur Miller, "Intention and Practical Reasoning," *Mind* 91 (1982): 106-108.

5. Thomas Baldwin, "Foresight and Responsibility," *Philosophy* 54 (1979): 347-360; George Graham, "Doing Something Intentionally and Moral Responsibility," *Canadian Journal of Philosophy* 11 (1981): 670-671; Arthur R. Miller, "Foresight, Intention and Responsibility," *Southern Journal of Philosophy* 27 (1989): 71-85.

6. Henry Benedict Tam, *A Philosophical Study of the Criteria for Responsibility Ascriptions: Responsibility and Personal Interactions* (Lewiston, NY: Edwin Mellen Press, 1990), 49.

7. *cf.* Harry G. Frankfurt, "Alternative Possibilities and Moral Responsibility," in *Moral Responsibility*, ed. John Martin Fischer (Ithaca, NY: Cornell University, 1986), 143-152; Peter Van Inwagen, "Ability and Responsibility," in *Moral Responsibility*, 153-173; John Martin Fischer, "Responsibility and Control," in *Moral Responsibility*, 174-190; May A. Webber, "No Moral Responsibility Without Alternative Possibilities," *Journal of Critical Analysis* 9 (1988): 27-34; George Schedler, "A Theory of Collective Responsibility and Some Applications," *Heythrop Journal* 23 (1982): 395-412.

8. For discussions on remoteness, *cf.* Hart and Honore, *Causation in the Law*, 397-401. On the notion of degrees of moral blameworthiness, *cf.* H. D. Lewis, "The Non-Moral Notion of Collective Responsibility," in *Individual and Collective Responsibility*, ed. French, 141; Virginia Held, "Moral Responsibility and Collective Action" in *Individual and Collective Responsibility*, 116; Robert Audi, "Moral Responsibility, Freedom, and Compulsion," *American Philosophical Quarterly* 11 (January, 1974): 2; Gregory Mellema, *Individuals, Groups, and Shared Moral Responsibility* (New York: Peter Lang, 1988) chaps. 2, 3; Susan Wendell, "Oppression and Victimization: Choice and Responsibility," *Hypatia* 5 (1990): 19.

9. For more on sharing blame, *cf.* Mellema, *Individuals, Groups, and Shared Moral Responsibility,* 7-8, 22-24, chaps. 2, 3.

10. Timothy Egan, "Elements of Tanker Disaster: Drinking, Fatigue, Complacency," *The New York Times,* 22 May 1989, B7. The importance of establishing blameworthiness in this case and some of the issues in doing so are addressed by William Joseph Frey, "Moral Responsibility and the *Exxon Valdez,*" *Contemporary Philosophy* 13, no. 2 (1990): 8-13.

11. *Ibid.*

12. Reports on the initial courtroom trial of Captain Hazelwood, are listed in *The New York Times Index,* (1990) 1282-1283.

13. Such judgment of moral responsibility and blame should, of course, be made carefully in order to avoid scapegoating. P. Eddy Wilson's discussions of corporate scapegoating are enlightening in this connection. P. Eddy Wilson, "The Fiction of Corporate Scapegoating," *Journal of Business Ethics* 12 (1993): 779-784.

14. Egan, "Elements of Tanker Disaster: Drinking, Fatigue, Complacency."

15. *Ibid.*

16. Strict liability is the principle, which has limited application, that one is liable for penalties for a violation of a law regardless of whether one is at fault for that violation, or whether moral responsibility is established. Strict liability amounts to the exclusion of any extenuating circumstances that serve to excuse one from moral blame for the penalty. Joel Feinberg, *Doing and Deserving* (Princeton: Princeton University, 1970), 223-225.

17. The fact that punishment which is directed against a group or organization as a whole has uneven effects on its members was clearly understood by H. D. Lewis, "The Non-Moral Notion of Collective Responsibility," *Individual and Collective Responsibility,* ed. French, 126-128.

18. Efforts to clarify degrees of blameworthiness, even in full knowledge of all individual participation or causal part in some wrong, are notoriously difficult and do not always admit of full, clear resolution, as Larry May has pointed out. Larry May, *Sharing Responsibility,* (Chicago: University of Chicago, 1992), 39. However, the point here is that even in the clearest imaginable case, there is no good purpose served by blaming an organization instead of the known culprits.

19. H. D. Lewis, "Collective Responsibility," in *Collective Responsibility,* ed. May and Hoffman, 17-18; Hannah Arendt, "Organized Guilt and Universal Responsibility," in *Collective Responsibility,* 273-283; Candace Hetzner, "Why We Mean What We Say: The History and Use of 'Corporate Social Responsibility'," *Business and Professional Ethics Journal* 6, no.3 (1987): 26.

20. This is a strategy sometimes pursued successfully by corporations in legal cases. Andrew M. Colman, "Crowd Psychology in South African Murder Trials," *American Psychologist* 46 (1991): 1071-9; Daniel Pearl, "Georgia-Pacific Pleads Guilty To Tax Evasion," *The Wall Street Journal*, 3 October, 1991, A3.

21. Peter A. French, "Principles of Responsibility, Shame and the Corporation," in *Shame, Responsibility and the Corporation,* ed. Curtler, 17-55.

# Chapter 2

## Evidence that an Organization Deserves Moral Blame

The first chapter explored many of the purposes of blaming and some of their implications. The present chapter examines the evidence adduced to support claims that an organization is to blame. The purpose of this chapter is to identify the conditions under which it makes sense to attribute moral blame to an organization.

Chapter one set forth the initial case for the thesis of individual sufficiency: that there is no significant moral purpose served by blaming an organization for something if we know all the moral blame deserved by all the responsible individuals. This thesis has an important consequence: in order for it to be significant to blame an organization, there must be some inadequacy in our knowledge of how much blame is deserved by which individuals for the matter at hand.

If blaming an organization requires an inadequacy in our knowledge of individual blame, how great an inadequacy must this be? Can it be so great that we have no knowledge that any personnel in the organization deserve the slightest bit of blame for the matter at hand? That is, could there be good reason to blame an organization if in fact we had no evidence whatsoever that any personnel in the organization were in any way blameworthy for the matter at hand? What if it had turned out that the *Exxon Valdez* had gone aground due to the failure of some equipment, and this failure was entirely fortuitous and staggeringly improbable, not due to inadequate policies, procedures, actual work performance or attention to duty by any individuals in the organization? Could it be worthwhile to blame any organizations for the grounding? The present chapter argues that the most plausible answer is, "No," that such blame could not be reasonable in such circumstances.

The thesis that it is unjustifiable to blame an organization without evidence that some of its personnel are to some extent blameworthy is referred to as the thesis of individual dependency. It implies that cogent organizational blame requires the blameworthiness of some of its personnel. It is a view that can be best understood in contrast to the influential work of Peter French.[1]

## 2.1 Separating Corporate from Individual Blame

French maintains that a corporation can be morally blameworthy for some matter even if none of its human constituents are morally blameworthy for it in any contributory ways.[2] He holds this view as a result of a well-developed argument showing that corporations can be moral agents, which he calls "persons."[3] Corporations can be moral agents because they can have intentionality--that is, they can be described literally as making decisions and acting intentionally. Moreover, that intentionality cannot be accounted for by the intentions of the individuals associated through the corporation. It is the fact that the corporation has what French calls an "internal decision structure" that is the source of its moral personhood, not the fact that it is comprised of individual, human, moral persons.

An internal decision structure is a complex of rules, procedures, roles and customs by which individuals associated through the corporation arrive at a single decision allowed to guide its policy and actions. Outcomes of the functioning of the decision structure delineate the will of the corporation. This will is such that no one member of the corporation need fully agree with it. But the corporation intends its policy decisions to be carried out by its personnel, who in fact do so on pain of losing their positions in the corporation. These individuals act to carry out their parts and, in doing so, the corporation acts. That is, their actions are performed to further corporate policy, and in doing so may be redescribed as actions of the corporation, intended by it, but for which it but not necessarily any of its constituents is morally responsible.[4]

French holds explicitly that something accurately can be described as morally blameworthy only if it has intentions, can act and decide in typically intentional ways, and thus has moral personhood. Since a corporation has its own unique decision structure through which the roles of the humans in it are subordinated, homogenized, and transformed, the corporation has intentions, and acts in ways that differ from any particular combination of the intentions or actions of its personnel. The specific nature of many corporate policies and the fact that many or even all of the personnel in the organization may disagree with these policies can only be fully understood by grasping the ways in which they result from the functioning of an internal decision structure.

French explains repeatedly how it is possible that no individuals in the corporation have intentions that match those attributable to the corporation.[5] He concludes that the corporation can have a moral responsibility that is different from that of any of its individuals. French's argument at this point does not, however, establish the falsehood of the dependency thesis. For two theses to be different or distinct does not prove that one does not depend for its plausibility upon the presence of the other. Claims of corporate blameworthiness may depend for their plausibility upon the fact that some individuals are blameworthy.

Before noting French's argument against the dependency thesis, it is instructive to note that he does not reject two other theses of logical dependence regarding concepts that are closely allied to that of moral responsibility. He does not deny that the presence of organizational intentions may presuppose individual intentions, or that organizational action may presuppose individual action. The reasons he does not are instructive.

Consider the relationship between organizational and individual intentions. First, French does not suggest that a corporation can have a given intention without its personnel having certain appropriate intentions. One can readily state good reasons for his not doing so. If the actual intentions of the personnel contradicted the supposed intentions of the corporation, there would be serious question as to just what the actual intentions of the corporation were. Suppose one brought forth some memos and other corporate documents implying or stating goals contradicting those of all the personnel. One might be inclined to say that those memos do not express the actual present corporate intent.

Second, French does not suggest that an organization can have intentions if its personnel have no intentions. He states, "Corporate intentions are always reducible to such executive intentions."[6] The existence of corporate intentions requires the existence of some appropriate intentions of corporate personnel. Assertions about corporate intentions presuppose (and thus depend upon) the existence of certain appropriate (and thus contributing) individual human intentions.

Consider next the relationship between organizational action and individual action. French does not argue that corporations could act to any significant extent if none of their constituent individuals act in ways that contribute appropriately.[7] Rather, he holds explicitly that corporate acts and individual acts are "causally inseparable."[8] Of course, individual actions may be differentiated from the actions of the corporation and are describable independently of them. But French allows that attributing corporate action presupposes the possibility of attributing contributory, cooperative, appropriate actions on the part of some corporate personnel.

Virginia Held has put forward an objection to French's view on the relationship between individual and corporate action. She cites an imaginary case which might appear to be an exception to his position. She describes a corporation that emits toxic, fish-killing chemicals into a river after all humans have perished from the earth. She then asserts that the corporation may be said to be killing fish.[9] Held appears to hold that a corporation could properly be said to act to kill even if no humans perform contributory actions. She appears to hold that the mere functioning of the machinery set in motion by a corporation can be described as the corporation acting.

The problem with the objection is that it may play on an ambiguity in the word "kill." While it is true that people can kill intentionally, it is also true that the forces of nature, such as lightning, can be said to kill. However, it would be strange to say that the corporation is intentionally killing fish or that it is acting to kill fish. Its machinery is killing fish because of the way humans previously set it up. Thus, the corporation is not, in any ordinary sense, performing the intentional act of killing fish.

If French can accept a thesis of logical dependence defined in terms of corporate and individual intentions and corporate and individual actions, why, then, does he in fact reject the corresponding thesis about individual and corporate moral responsibility and thus blame? The answer is that he holds that a corporation is itself a moral person. Just as a human can be morally blameworthy, although no particular parts of it, such as its arms or legs are, so can a corporation be blameworthy independently of its parts, which happen to include human beings. French holds that a corporation can be morally blameworthy in the same way and for the very same kinds of reasons that a human person can. These reasons do not require anything in particular of the constituents of the whole thing.

## 2.2 The Thesis of Individual Dependency

The problem with French's position stems from the difference between the moral nature of human persons on the one hand and organizations with internal decision structures on the other. It is because some of their parts are moral persons that such organizations can serve plausibly as objects of moral blame. To attribute blame to an organization presupposes some contributory blameworthiness on the part of some of its personnel. Unless we presuppose that blameworthiness and thus grant the truth of the thesis of individual dependency, attributing blame to an organization is no different from attributing blame to a machine or computer. It is a suggestive, colorful, anthropomorphic expression, but it lacks moral force.

Two arguments supporting the dependency thesis are developed below. Each emerges from examination of French's position that a corporation can be blameworthy although none of its personnel are. One objection to this position, formulated in A., is that blaming a corporation while exonerating all of its personnel is incoherent. The second, formulated in B., denies the plausibility of French's view that a corporation may be blameworthy although all of its personnel have exculpatory excuses.

## A. Blameworthy Corporations with Blameless Personnel

Consider French's thesis that to attribute blame to a corporation presupposes that it is a moral being. French argues that its moral nature lies in the fact that it is an intentional being capable of decisions and intentional actions. The fact that it has an internal decision structure is what allows it to be a single, intentional, and moral being.

The problem here is that a decision structure cannot, alone, establish moral being. A decision structure includes the corporate charter, the complex of rules, responsibilities, power structures, lines of authority and procedures that regulate the inner workings of the corporation.[10] It is an inanimate framework within which corporate processes function, but it is not, itself, an intentional entity. The framework must be followed, given content, and thus used.

This framework cannot be a source of moral status if it is used only by a group of inanimate and nonintentional machines.[11]   And French has no inclination to rest his thesis on the contentious view that computers or other machinery can be truly intentional in a moral sense and thus have moral personhood. For French, what makes a corporation have intentionality in the full-bodied sense, and thus have a moral status beyond that of a mere machine, is the fact that its processes are largely initiated, directed, and carried out by real, live, human persons. It appears that on French's account, figuratively speaking, the corporation has moral status because the moral quality of the persons in it spreads out, passing to the corporation through their use of the corporate decision structures. Now if this figurative grasp of his view is accurate, it would seem that the moral status of a corporation from moment to moment depends upon the moral status of its personnel. For it to have the moral status of personhood, there must be humans present in it who also have this moral status. These points are reflected in an examination of the language of moral blame.

Consider an attribution of corporate blame together with the admission that no corporate personnel share in this blame in any way at all. Such a pair of statements, if uttered together, would contain an inner absurdity. For the pair implies that there is no moral reason for any corporate personnel at all to be concerned with the practices which demonstrate moral blameworthiness. Since none of them are to blame, none of them did wrong. And if so, then there is no moral reason for them to have tried to change things. Of course, they might have decided to change things, and we might now try to convince them that in the future, there are reasons why they should in such cases. But the fact that they did not do so was not a failure in any moral sense. Since they are not morally to blame for their past performance, there is no moral reason for them to think of it as inadequate, or in moral need of revising in similar situations in the future. We may accuse them of practical blindness and stupidity, but not of immorality.

To blame the corporation while exonerating all of its personnel would be self-defeating.  It would be self-defeating because it would say that although the corporation is to blame, none of its personnel are.  None of them need to be concerned for any moral reasons about what happened.  It just did, and if they ignore similar situations in the future, they will not be morally to blame for these sorts of things happening then any more than they are morally to blame now.

This is self-defeating because of its implications for those who are most centrally located in regard to the untoward matter in question, and thus most able to have acted to prevent it.  To blame the corporation and exonerate the personnel tells those people that they need not be morally concerned.  Yet one of the most important purposes of such blame is precisely to send a message, that all the people who can, do have a moral obligation to put more effort into preventing such matters from happening in the future.   To blame the corporation but exonerate its personnel would be to pull the teeth from the act of blaming.   As French recognizes, corporations can only see, hear, think, decide, and act through their personnel.[12]  If blaming a corporation is to have any significance, it must send a forceful moral message to some of its personnel.  It can do so only if some of those personnel are also to blame.

There is, moreover, reason to think that whenever a corporation is blameworthy in the moral sense French advocates, so are some of its personnel.  For if its personnel constitute its eyes, ears, mind, will, and moving force, then if a corporation should have done otherwise, some of its personnel should have done something other than they did.  To separate their blameworthiness entirely from its blameworthiness, as French has done, is to ignore and contradict the significance of blaming the corporation.

## B. Excuses of Corporate Personnel

A second way to illuminate the problem with French's position is to examine some of the implications of one of his statements separating corporate and individual blameworthiness.  He states, "when a [corporation] is found morally responsible for some event, ...even all human beings associated with the [corporation] may have exculpatory excuses."[13]  Examination of the nature of some of these is telling.

They may have several possible exculpatory excuses.  They may argue: (1) that they did not have contributory moral duties to ensure that the corporation fulfilled its duty, (2) that they did not intend or expect the corporation to do what it did, or (3) that they could not prevent it from doing what it did.  There are important implications of each of these three that point to the need to assume that someone in the corporation must be blameworthy.

Consider the first possible excuse of organizational personnel, that they had no contributory moral duties to ensure that the corporation fulfilled its moral duty. Returning to a different aspect of the oil spill in the Prince William Sound may help clarify the salient points. Consider the question of who is to blame for the magnitude of the ecological disaster that followed from the oil spill by the *Exxon Valdez.* Suppose that Exxon corporate personnel insisted individually that none of them had a moral duty to act in any way differently than they did before and after the accident. If none of them had such a duty, who did? The facts of the case showed that Exxon had eliminated from its staff, two years before, nine oil spill specialists; that it had 69 barrels of dispersant on hand for a job requiring ten thousand; and that it had never tested its twenty-eight volume crisis management plan, which, it had boasted, would allow it to contain a spill within five hours.[14] Now French might reply that because it is a moral person, Exxon had duties to act differently. It and it alone may be at fault for these failures. That is, the corporation may have a moral duty while its personnel have no corresponding moral duty to ensure that its moral duty is carried out. The moral duties of its personnel are, for French, entirely irrelevant to its moral duty.

Such a position is not plausible because such a supposed corporate moral duty may be vacuous. A primary purpose of attributing such a moral duty to a corporation is to indicate to certain personnel within the corporation that they should ensure that its duties are fulfilled. But why should they? Should they do so for moral or for nonmoral reasons? If they have no such contributory duties, then there is no moral reason why they should act to ensure that the supposed duties of the corporation are fulfilled.

In that case, the only reasons they should act accordingly are nonmoral reasons. Now such reasons are contingent upon any number of factors, such as the directions of their superiors, or the fact that their job descriptions include a mandate to act to ensure that the corporation fulfills its moral duties. If such mandate is lacking in the corporate environment, then they need not be concerned. If neither their superiors nor their job descriptions direct them to act accordingly, they then have no reason whatever to ensure that the corporation fulfill its moral duties. And if this is the case, then the corporation supposedly has a moral duty although no one has any reason whatsoever to ensure that it fulfill that duty.

This is, of course, absurd. It is gratuitous to assert that a corporation has a moral duty, but that there is no reason at all why anyone in the corporation should act to ensure that it fulfill that duty. To assert such a thing would be to pull the teeth from the attribution of a moral duty.

The important point here is that moral obligations are obligations which exist whether or not anyone directs others to recognize them. In separating corporate duties from individual duties, French allows the absurd possibility that individuals may have no reason to contribute to the fulfillment of the corporate moral duties. By allowing that there may be no reason to contribute to such duties, such a position robs the supposed corporate moral duties of their moral significance. Yet the significance of such duties is precisely that they give human individuals significant reason to act in certain ways. There can be little moral force to a claim that a corporation has a duty while acknowledging at the same time that its personnel have no contributory duties.

A second possible exculpatory excuse for Exxon personnel may be that they neither intended nor expected such a huge spill to occur. The corporation may be blameworthy although they are not. The problem here is that the personnel can be morally blameworthy for things which they did not intend or anticipate. They might still be blameworthy because they failed to fulfill a moral duty to try to anticipate such major environmental disasters caused by their tankers. So the second excuse may fail to show that none of the corporate personnel are in fact blameless. Some may be blameworthy even though none intended or expected the disaster to occur.

A third possible exculpatory excuse is that none of the constituents of the organization, by using normal human foresight and then working effectively within the corporate structure, could have prevented the ecological disaster. This, however, is unlikely. It is unlikely that if the organization is morally responsible for something, precautions could not have been taken or should not be anticipated by a concerted effort of some combination of its constituents.

If, on the other hand, it is really, finally true that no corporate personnel could reasonably be expected to have taken more likely effective and affordable steps to plan for the spill, there is a further implication. In such a case, the corporation may well itself be exculpated, and not deserve blame. If we accept the dictum that "ought implies can" as essential for moral blame, then if corporate personnel could not have taken precautionary measures, the corporation could not be to blame. For the corporation does not have some higher level of abilities independent of or over and above those of the coordinated actions of its personnel.

The centrality of individuals to cases of corporate blameworthiness and the presence of evidence that some individuals are likely to blame is strikingly apparent throughout the cases French discusses. To argue that corporate policies and procedures were at fault for an airplane crash, as French does, suggests to any thoughtful reader the question of which corporate executives oversaw the administration of them.[15]

To contradict French's position and affirm the dependency thesis does not prove that a corporation cannot have characteristics of moral personhood. But the analysis that supports this thesis does indicate the presence of a close connection between the blameworthiness of an organization and that of its constituents. And this connection is closer than French's position allows.

It is only because an organization is made up of human persons that it can plausibly be blamed. The presence of those persons is a necessary condition for attributions of corporate moral personhood. And the blameworthiness of some of those persons, whether or not we know exactly who they are, or just how blameworthy they may be, is a necessary condition for plausible attributions of organizational moral blame.

One important implication of the dependency thesis is that the morally blameworthy organization is not some entity that is totally independent of its personnel. In attributing moral responsibility to a conglomerate, one implicates, however indefinitely, at least some of those individuals. If one cannot name them specifically, one at least presupposes the possibility of doing so.

## 2.3 Sharpening the Thesis of Individual Dependency

The thesis of individual sufficiency and the thesis of individual dependency state two necessary conditions for blaming an organization. However, as addressed to this point, these two have a different nature. The first is a condition of evidence, and the second a condition of being. Sufficiency requires that in order to blame meaningfully, one not possess complete evidence of all the responsible individuals. So far, however, dependency does not appear to require the presence of any evidence of any kind. It simply presupposes that some individuals, though perhaps unknown, deserve some blame for their parts in the matter at hand. It does not, as yet, appear to require that one have evidence of any such individual blame. In fact, however, there is reason to think that it does require such evidence.

There are two interpretations of the thesis that attributions of organizational blame presuppose evidence of individual blame. One interpretation is that there must be evidence that some specific individuals are to blame, and the other is that there must be evidence that some individuals are to blame, even if there is no clear indication who they are. The first interpretation does not yield a necessary condition for blaming an organization, but the second does.

Returning once again to the ecological disaster in the Prince William Sound, consider the possibility that no individuals are found to be blameworthy in any respect for the failure to contain the spill, once the ship had hit bottom. If this is the case, then the spreading oil can be accounted for in one of two ways. Either it occurred (A) because of a combination of chance occurrences that proved to be unpredictable and uncontrollable by normal, responsible, conscientious people; or (B) because there is evidence that something went wrong, someone should have done something differently, but we simply do not have any clear or plausible evidence of which individuals share the blame.

If A was the case, then no people were in fact blameworthy at all, and, for reasons discussed in 2.2, the case could not support the moral blameworthiness of Exxon. Such a finding, then, would not contradict the dependency thesis.

If, on the other hand, B was the case, then, as in A, we also lack evidence of any specific individuals who are to blame. Now could we have, in such a case, evidence sufficient to warrant a claim of organizational blame? Note that such limited evidence was exactly what was possessed by the National

Transportation Safety Board after its investigation concluded by May 22, 1989, two months after the accident. That is, the Board had evidence that measures had not been taken that might well have significantly reduced the environmental damage from the spill. But it had very limited information about who in Exxon might be to blame for the lack of such measures.

Whether or not anyone really is to blame is not, here, the issue. The question is whether we might have evidence that some organization is to blame, and yet lack evidence that any specific individuals are to blame. It seems clear that this might well occur. There might well be evidence that Exxon had failed, that surely some of its personnel should have done more, but that we just do not at the moment have good evidence of who it was, or just what duties they shirked, and how. So the dependency thesis cannot clearly be strengthened to assert that evidence that some specifically identified individuals are to blame is a necessary condition for blaming an organization.

The case is different on the second interpretation of the question. In order to blame an organization on plausible grounds, must one have evidence that some of its individuals are blameworthy, even if no evidence of just who they are? There are important reasons to think that one must.

Consider the prior analysis of the ecological disaster in the Prince William Sound, and the question of whether one could have evidence of organizational blameworthiness without evidence that any individuals at all were likely blameworthy. How, that is, could there be evidence that Exxon is blameworthy without evidence that some people are to blame as well? It seems clear that any evidence at all of the company's blameworthiness would also offer evidence of human blameworthiness. Records of policies, procedures, memos, letters, and personal testimony would all, if taken to implicate the company's blameworthiness, unavoidably point to that of individuals, even if it is not clear exactly who they were or just how blameworthy they are.

What sort of evidence could show that an organization is to blame while offering no evidence of the contributory blameworthiness of individual personnel? Such information would have to lack any reason to think that humans could and should have taken precautionary steps. In that case, the organization just did, due to nothing that anyone should have changed, function in a way producing some wrong. If so, then blaming it would be similar to blaming Mother Nature for a fatal strike of lightning. Such blame would lack moral force for human beings and human life. It would lack a moral purpose beyond that of expressing frustration with the forces of nature or fate.

In conclusion, then, we can formulate the thesis of individual dependency to include a requirement about the evidence which one must have in order to blame an organization. This thesis has two parts.

*The Thesis of Individual Dependency*

A. In order for an organization to be blameworthy for some matter, some individuals in it must share some blame for their contribution to it.

B. Evidence sufficient to provide cogent support for the claim that an organization is to blame must include evidence that some of its personnel are to blame, even if it is unclear who they are or to what extent they are to blame.

The ensuing discussion is based largely on version B of the dependency Thesis. Taken together, the thesis of individual sufficiency and the thesis of individual dependency have important implications for understanding the blameworthiness of organizations. These two theses mark outer limits of the evidence for attributions of organizational blame. They indicate that there can be too much evidence for such attributions, and too little.

According to sufficiency, if we know all the individuals who are to blame, there is no significant purpose to blaming an organization. According to dependency, if one is to blame an organization justifiably, then one must have evidence that there are some individuals in it who share the blame. Thus, to blame an organization presupposes that one has evidence that some, but not all, of its personnel share some blame for their parts in contributing to the untoward matter in question.

## 2.4 Individuals in Organizations

Evidence to support a claim that an organization is to blame requires more than the evidence specified by the sufficiency and dependency theses. It requires evidence that supports the plausibility of an organizational basis of this blameworthiness. One does not, of course, blame an organization simply because some of its personnel are blameworthy for something. Instead, there must be an intimate connection between the individuals and the nature of their blameworthiness and their relationships through the organization. There must be evidence that it was their places, roles, duties, actions or practices within the organization which reveal that they are to blame. That is, in order to attribute blame to the organization, there must be evidence that some of its personnel, acting through the organizational framework, were morally negligent.

The personnel of the organization are related to one another through the network of organizational relationships. They have certain duties defined by their places in the organization. Those places are defined by the goals, rules, policies, standard practices, and even the "corporate culture" of the organization. The goals of the personnel are to carry these out, and their acts and practices are described as the acts and practices of the organization in so far as their acts and practices are directed to further the main goals of the organization. Blame is attributed to the organization when it is organizational interrelationships (such as roles, policies, practices, procedures, goals) of various kinds that likely play an essential role in the individuals' blameworthiness.

In order for the organization to be considered blameworthy, one need not view its personnel as directly to blame for the actual matter itself. Thus, if Exxon is to blame for failing to test its oil cleanup plans, it need not be the case that any particular managers are to blame for failing to test the plans. It is sufficient that some are to blame for their parts in the failure that led to this egregious omission.

Suppose that several managers had, individually, thought of conducting test runs to ensure that the oil cleanup plans would work smoothly. But suppose that they simply had these thoughts privately, and never discussed them with others, and never wrote memos to implement actual tests. In that case, they may well be to blame for their failures in the case. But due to the indirect nature of those failures, perhaps none of them deserve to be properly singled out as "to blame for the ecological disaster in the Prince William Sound." They may share in the blame for the disaster, but indirectly.

These points may be summarized as conditions of the evidence that is necessary in order for one to substantiate a claim of organizational blame:

A. There is evidence that some individuals who are blameworthy for contributing to the matter at hand were connected through a network of organizational relationships.

B. There is evidence that the individual blameworthiness arose within the organizational context partly in response to organizational goals, policies, or practices.

## 2.5 Five Conditions of Plausibility for Blaming Organizations

It is now possible to combine the conditions for individual moral blameworthiness from 1.1 with the sufficiency and dependency theses and finally the conditions of 2.4. This list is considered in the ensuing chapters as presenting a set of necessary conditions which, when all are satisfied, define the presence of a sufficient amount of evidence to warrant the claim that an organization is morally blameworthy for something.

To blame an organization on plausible grounds, one must have evidence that the following obtain:

1. Some matter (event, process, or state of affairs) came to be, and is morally objectionable. That is, some combination of people should (and could) have taken measures which would have prevented it from occurring. They had a moral duty to take those measures.

2. More people are blameworthy for having contributed to the matter at hand than any specific people whose blameworthiness is known.

3. A subset of those with a moral duty to take preventive measures were related through a network of organizational interrelationships.

4. Some of those in the subset could have taken appropriate measures to fulfill their relevant moral duties but did not, and have no good moral, exculpatory excuse for not having done so.

5. The dereliction of moral duty producing the matter in question arose within the context and as a result of the organizational interrelationships.

These are not put forth as necessary and sufficient conditions for the truth of statements of organizational blame. They do not define the evidence that would prove conclusively the truth of such statements. And there are other conditions that need to be present in order that one have conclusive proof that an organization is morally responsible for something. These are, at best, conditions of warranted assertibility. That is, if they are fulfilled, then one might make, plausibly, a claim that an organization is morally blameworthy. One would have reasonable, if not conclusive evidence for making the claim, and the claim would be intelligible under such conditions. If no further confirming or disconfirming evidence came in, one's claim might be respected as rational, even if some could still find grounds upon which to dispute it. One's claim might be rational in the sense that the purposes of making the claim are understandable and justifiable, and there is significant evidence for making it.

It is important to understand why fulfillment of the five conditions might not provide conclusive proof that an organization is to blame. First, fulfillment of them can only give inductive support to the view that the organization is to blame. It might, after all, turn out, given appropriate future evidence, that the organization is not to blame. There might have been within the organization a small group of employees who conspired to cause the problem, and are totally to blame for it. Second, one might reject the very plausibility, coherence, or meaningfulness of attributing moral blameworthiness to a corporation, as do some of those who dispute French's position.[16] Meaningful claims of organizational blameworthiness which fulfill the five conditions are inherently tentative.

It would misinterpret their import to object that people do at times make what pass for plausible attributions of blame to organizations without possessing evidence that these obtain. The fact that this occurs is no objection to them. They are an attempt of codify our well-considered intuitions, not to deny them. The point is not that we actually use these as a checklist to determine the plausibility of a claim. We often do not. The point is, rather, that we could, and that using them as a checklist would, in some circumstances, help us clarify our intuitions and determine whether our evidence can plausibly support blame directed at an organization.

Applying these conditions to a possible interpretation of the ecological disaster in the Prince William Sound illuminates the reasoning that might lead one conclude that Exxon is morally blameworthy. Beginning, as before, with the disaster caused by the spreading oil, one may note, in response to the first requirement, that such an occurrence should have been able to be forestalled by appropriate human response. That is, one might argue that this disaster was not some unpredictable quirk of nature, and that people could have had more effective plans in effect at the time. To have more adequate quantities of dispersant on hand, to have tested the company's plans, and to maintain an adequate number of oil cleanup experts on the staff would not have been unaffordably expensive for a corporation the size and wealth of Exxon. Furthermore, the magnitude of the disaster reveals how serious the matter was, and provides evidence that proper precautions would have been well worth the rather minimal expense.

Next, it is important to consider whether there was a moral duty for anyone to take steps to fund and implement appropriate preventive plans. Several approaches are relevant here. Environmentalists have argued that we have a moral duty to protect the environment. If so, then on whom does such a duty bear, and to what extent? On each citizen? Just what are their individual duties, and how should they carry them out? We normally refer to the legitimate organizations of society as means for carrying out the responsibilities of society. Specific duties are then allocated to those in the appropriate offices of these organizations. Such considerations might, in this case, lead us to consider the possibility that oil company managers had appropriate moral duties.

Assuming that we have established the likelihood that some such people have some such duties, one considers, third, whether anyone can be known to be blameworthy for the outcome. Here, three alternatives are worth considering. (A) Suppose, on the one hand, that almost all Exxon employees in appropriate positions asked the right questions and maintained an appropriate interest in the environmental planning and did what they reasonably could be expected to do to take the appropriate steps to prevent such a debacle. However, suppose that two Exxon managers in key positions ignored the questions and the recommendations of the other employees. Suppose these two procrastinated in doing their jobs, reported falsely that environmental planning was proceeding apace, and deliberately turned their backs on it. In such a case, one might be inclined to blame the whole disaster on these two, and avoid blaming Exxon, as required by the thesis of individual sufficiency.

(B) Suppose, on the other hand, that the two delinquent managers are identified and their roles in the matter clarified. Suppose, however, that the roles of these two are not sufficient to account for the magnitude of the problem. That is, full consideration of all the evidence in the case reveals that there was likely further neglect or human involvement in the matter beyond these two. Suppose, also, that evidence indicates that there were likely others who failed, for one reason or another, to ask the right questions and check on the two known blameworthy individuals. Such considerations would lead one to investigate the nature of their likely connections to the two, and to the disaster. One might then entertain the hypothesis that these others, although we may be unsure exactly who they are, are interconnected through various organizational ties, perhaps working in some environmental division of Exxon. We would then be inclined to search for evidence of organizational culture and various more subtle interrelationships which account for their neglect. We might, at this point, begin to consider the possibility that the overall organization, Exxon, should be blamed for the disaster. It might become increasingly likely, as we investigate the matter, that the environmental divisions had been encouraged by various echelons of the company to save money than to stockpile appropriate cleanup equipment.

(C) Suppose, finally, that we identify no clearly blameworthy individuals, but are left, instead, with a morass of vague information. Such information might include references to lost memos, managers turning their backs, employees resigning mysteriously, others being transferred to other positions after a few months, and so on. Such evidence may point to the likelihood of a lot of inadequate performance on the part of many individuals, but no clear culprits. We would likely be inclined to search for evidence that organizational interconnections among some unclearly identified group of blameworthy individuals might help explain their neglect. In doing so, we would then be searching for further evidence which might support a claim of organizational blame.

In order to support a claim of organizational blame in either scenario (B) or (C), we would need to determine that the last three of the five conditions are fulfilled. The third requires that we determine whether or not individuals having the relevant moral duties identified for the first condition are now or have ever been connected to Exxon. If no one within Exxon has such duties, there are no grounds here for blaming Exxon. If none of those who have such duties are Exxon personnel, or are connected with Exxon in any significant way, there is again a lack of grounds to blame Exxon. For in both cases, there is no known connection between the dereliction of duty of the likely blameworthy individuals and the organization. If, on the other hand, some of those with such duties are Exxon personnel, and they regularly perform within their organizational roles, we next determine whether they fulfilled their relevant moral duties, and if not, whether their organizational involvement played a significant role in their not doing so.

The fourth requirement, then, is that there is evidence that some of those within the organization who had the relevant moral duties could have fulfilled them but did not, and lack exculpatory excuses. Note that if they fulfilled their relevant moral duties, or if they have exculpatory excuses, then there is no good reason to think they are blameworthy, and no good reason as yet to blame the organization. Now this fourth requirement must be interpreted in light of the thesis of individual dependency. It does not require that we have evidence of any specific individuals who are blameworthy because they shirked their moral duties. But it does require that we have evidence that there are some individuals, however unclear their exact numbers or identities may be, who could have fulfilled their duties, should have, but did not, and have no known exculpatory excuses. Thus, there may be evidence that some Exxon personnel turned their backs on the relevant issues whenever they arose.

The fifth and final requirement for blaming the organization is that the dereliction of moral duty which led to the ecological disaster resulted from various organizational interrelationships. Although conclusive evidence of this is not always forthcoming, there may well be significant amounts of evidence pointing in this direction. There could be evidence, for example, that managers had talked about implementing the plans, but that severe budget cuts likely had made an impact on their thinking. Much of the kinds of evidence discussed above might contribute to the case here.

If these five conditions have all been fulfilled, then why blame the organization? Why not simply say that some indefinite group of personnel in Exxon were likely responsible for the ecological disaster? This, after all, is what the evidence shows.

The disadvantage of blaming some indefinite group of individuals is that doing so does not put the emphasis where it might seem the emphasis belongs. And this is the likely fact, given (B) and (C), that it was many people who played a part, and that it was due to some interrelationships of the organization in which they participated that the ecological disaster occurred. In blaming an organization, one may be offering an explanation about the basis and genesis of human blameworthiness in the case. One may be asserting that the blameworthiness can be traced to a complex set of human interrelationships that are best understood in the context of an organization through which they develop and influence people's lives.

Instead of blaming an organization, one might choose to blame an indefinite group of personnel in the organization. However, to do this is to state far less than that for which we have evidence. For we have evidence that the personnel are blameworthy, and that this is due in part to certain organizational interrelationships. We can suggest ways that such blameworthiness can be avoided in the future. By stating that the organization is to blame, we may be suggesting that careful attention should be paid to the functioning of the organization and to the kinds of influence it exerts on people. Perhaps we should consider checks and balances on all aspects of such organizations, and not simply leave them to function on their own.

## 2.6 Some Tentative Answers

The five conditions and the account they suggest offer a basis for some tentative answers to some of the questions about blaming an organization which were raised in 1.2. These included questions of the object of such blame, what evidence is needed to establish such blame, and the motives for blaming. Recall that similar questions, when addressed to the blaming of a group of people, such as the Lions fans, could be answered in rather straightforward ways. For such a group, one may attribute blame to some or all of its members, depending on the intentions of the speaker. Such blame is warranted if there is sufficient evidence that those members are to blame. The purposes of blaming in such a case pose no special problems apart from those which motivate the blaming of individuals.

Attributing blame to an organization is, however, different. As the sufficiency thesis reveals, there is no significant purpose to blaming an organization when there is full evidence that its personnel are to blame. In that case, we do better to blame the individuals. Yet, as dependency reveals, in order to blame an organization, there must be some evidence that some of its personnel are to blame. What, then, is sufficient evidence for blaming an organization?

The conditions for doing so specified above in 2.5 indicate, in sum, that there must be plausible evidence that some of the organization's personnel share some blame for the matter at hand; but the evidence must be insufficient to establish just which individuals in the organization deserve all the blame. Moreover, there must be evidence that the blameworthiness of the likely individuals arose in the context of their organizational commitments, capacities and various interrelationships.

The five conditions do not require that there is a single entity to which organizational blame is attributed. Nor do they offer any basis for a claim, such as that of Peter French, that an organization is a moral agent or person. However, as explored further in chapter six, neither do they contradict in toto the possibility that one may intend an attribution of organizational blame to refer to an organization conceived of as a moral person. They allow, but do not require, that in blaming an organization, we may intend or be construed as attributing blame to an indefinite group of individuals connected through organizational ties. The five conditions do not require that attributions of organizational blame be understood as purely referring expressions. As addressed in chapters three and four, they may have a more complex and subtle meaning. There may be a similarity here to statements that two people have a strong marriage. The two people do not literally have a thing that is a marriage. To say they have a strong marriage is to make a statement about the ways they relate to one another. Similarly, to say an organization is to blame is not necessarily to say that there is some abstract person to blame. It may mean, rather, that some individuals are to blame; they are related through an organizational network; that for which they are to blame has been influenced by that network; and some combination of organizational personnel should have done something to modify this environment to ensure that such things would not happen. To name the organization as the culprit may be to specify the organizational milieu as playing a central role in what led to the matters in question. It may suggest the likely blameworthiness of some indefinite number of significant organizational personnel in positions of potential or actual power. It may serve as a shorthand way of attributing moral responsibility in the presence of complex human relationships and conditions of uncertainty.

Why, then, blame the organization? One may do so for any of the eight purposes addressed in 1.6, and perhaps for more. The eighth purpose may, however, be more typical than initially appears. We may attribute such blame when we find ourselves in a situation with incomplete information about individual blameworthiness, but evidence that some contributory individual blameworthiness stems from the roles and relationships of individuals in an organization. We may attribute blame in a figurative way to something called "the organization" because it is through its network of goals, policies and practices that the real human blame must be understood. Blaming the organization may be a shorthand way of stating the hypothesis that those properly to blame are in some indefinite group of individuals whose blameworthiness results from their connections through the organization.

The five conditions shed light on the questions raised in 1.2 about blaming an architectural firm for the collapse of a part of the stadium it designed. Certain questions were noted about the meaning of such blame and what evidence could justify it. Would one mean that the whole firm was to blame, or just the morally culpable architects? What could it mean to attribute blame to the firm? What evidence could one adduce to prove that it is most appropriate to attribute blame to the firm instead of to some of its personnel? And just why would one be inclined to blame the firm instead of simply the morally culpable architects within it?

The present analysis suggests answers such as the following: there is evidence that some within the firm are to blame, even if we are unsure who they are. One may anticipate that evidence will show that this part of the stadium was poorly designed, and that some architects within the firm are, in some typically moral sense, to blame.  But beyond this, the blameworthiness of some individual engineers is not yet known, but likely occurred in an organizational milieu.  There should have been safeguards built into the design processes of the firm to ensure that no faulty designs would be sold.  Some leading partners of the firm may be to blame if there is a lack of such checks or quality control.  It may never be entirely clear just who is to blame, to what extent and for exactly what, even if all the facts come to be known.  But the most likely blameworthy individuals are personnel within the firm, and their connections through the firm were likely essential to their blameworthiness.  If so, it may make good sense to blame the firm in the presence of rather indefinite individual blameworthiness.  In doing so, one may be attributing blame to an indefinite number of individuals connected through the firm, who are blameworthy due in part to that connection.

## 2.7 Chapter Summary

The thesis of individual sufficiency, explored in chapter one, reveals that blaming an organization serves no significant purpose unless there is some inadequacy in our knowledge of blame deserved by individuals for the matter at hand.  To determine how great of an inadequacy this must be, the first three sections of the chapter examined the question of whether we could justifiably blame an organization if no individuals in it deserved any blame at all for failing to take steps to prevent the matter.  The question was divided into two parts.  First is the issue of whether one can, as French thinks, plausibly blame an organization while at the same time acknowledging that none of its personnel are in any way to blame.  Such a position is implausible because it contradicts the purpose and significance of blaming an organization.  In addition, if all personnel actually do have legitimate exculpatory excuses, then so does the organization.

The second aspect of the question is that of whether one could have evidence that an organization is to blame if one had no evidence at all that some of its personnel are blameworthy for their contribution to the matter.  Here, it appeared that any evidence for the blameworthiness of the organization will include evidence for the blameworthiness of some of its personnel.  The answer to the question was then formulated as the thesis of individual dependency: that in order to blame an organization, one must assume that some of its personnel have some contributory blameworthiness, and one must have evidence that some do, even if it is not clear which ones do.

The sufficiency and dependency theses are then combined with conditions for individual blameworthiness and further conditions regarding the relationship of individuals to organizations to offer a set of conditions that are necessary and may be, in some cases, together sufficient to justify one's attributing blame to an organization. One may do so when, in short, there is evidence that some of its personnel share some contributory blame for the matter at hand, there is a lack of evidence of all the blame deserved by all the individuals who deserve blame for the matter, and evidence that the personnel deserve blame due in part to their roles within the organization. We may blame organizations when we have incomplete evidence, and that evidence indicates individual blameworthiness resulting in part from organizational interconnections and influences.

## Notes

1. Peter A. French, "The Corporation as a Moral Person," *American Philosophical Quarterly* 16 (1979): 207-215; Peter A. French, *Collective and Corporate Responsibility* (New York: Columbia University, 1984); Peter A. French, "Principles of Responsibility, Shame and the Corporation," in *Shame, Responsibility and the Corporation*, ed. Curtler, chap. 1, 19-55.

2. French, *Collective and Corporate Responsibility*, 15. Others have joined French in denying the Dependency Thesis; *cf.* Patricia H. Werhane, *Persons, Rights and Corporations* (Englewood Cliffs, NJ: Prentice-Hall, 1985), 56; Mellema, *Individuals, Groups, and Shared Moral Responsibility*, 8, 15, 27.

3. French, *Collective and Corporate Responsibility*, 29, 38-47; French, "Principles of Responsibility, Shame and the Corporation," in *Shame, Responsibility and the Corporation*, ed. Curtler, 36.

4. French, *Collective and Corporate Responsibility*, chaps. 2, 3.

5. *Ibid.,* 41-47.

6. *Ibid.,* 40-41.

7. For a searching formal analysis of this point, see David Copp, "Collective Actions and Secondary Actions," *American Philosophical Quarterly* 16 (1979).

8. French, *Collective and Corporate Responsibility*, 42.

9. Held, "Corporations, Persons, and Responsibility," in *Shame, Responsibility and the Corporation*, ed. Curtler, 170.

10. French, *Collective and Corporate Responsibility*, 43-45.

11. The argument developed here was suggested by the comments of Lewis, Held and David Ozar. Lewis, "Collective Responsibility," in *Collective Responsibility,* ed. May and Hoffman, 28; Held, "Moral Responsibility and Collective Action," in *Individual and Collective Responsibility,* ed. French, 115; David T. Ozar, "Do Corporations Have Moral Rights?," *Journal of Business Ethics* 4 (1985): 277-281.

12. French, *Collective and Corporate Responsibility,* 45.

13. *Ibid.,* 16.

14. Claudia H. Deutsch, "The Giant With a Black Eye," *The New York Times* 2 April 1989, sec. 3, 1; Steven Fink, "Prepare for Crisis, It's Part of Business," *The New York Times* 30 April 1989, sec. 3, 3; Egan, "Elements of Tanker Disaster: Drinking, Fatigue, Complacency," *The New York Times,* 22 May 1989, B7.

15. French, *Collective and Corporate Responsibility,* chap. 10. This point has been well noted by Jan Edward Garrett, "Unredistributable Corporate Moral Responsibility," *Journal of Business Ethics* 8 (1989): 538-539.

16. *cf.* Phillips, "Corporate Moral Personhood and Three Conceptions of the Corporation," *Business Ethics Quarterly* 2 (1992): 435-459; Jeffrey Nesteruk, "The Moral Status of the Corporation: Comments on an Inquiry," *Business Ethics Quarterly* 2, (1992): 461-464; R. E. Ewin, "The Moral Status of the Corporation," *Journal of Business Ethics* 10, (1991): 749-756; Nicholas J. Caste, "Corporations and Rights," *Journal of Value Inquiry* 26, no. 2, (1992): 199-209; R. M. Barlow, "Corporations as Ethical Persons," *Contemporary Philosophy* 13, no. 3, (1990): 10-14; Otto Neumaier, "Are Collectives Morally Responsible?," in *Advances in Scientific Philosophy: Essays in Honour of Paul Weingartner,* ed., Gerhard Schurz and Georg J. W. Dorn, (Atlanta, GA: Rodopi, 1991), 495-516.

# Chapter 3

## Problems for Dependency?

The sufficiency and dependency theses and the five conditions based on them are established in the first two chapters as answers to certain specific questions and by reference to a few cases that are called forth by those questions. There are, however, other questions to be raised about blaming organizations and other cases that have been and should be brought forth for consideration. If the present analysis is successful, it should be able to provide plausible answers to those questions and clear, consistent accounts of those cases. The present chapter addresses a number of such cases and questions. Consideration of them sharpens the analyses of the first two chapters.

### 3.1 Blaming an Organization When the Culprits Are Gone

The thesis of individual dependency requires that in order to attribute moral blame to an organization, there must be evidence that someone in the organization is partially blameworthy for the untoward matter at hand. Such a thesis appears to ignore the fact that personnel come and go from organizations, and that organizations may be blamed for something even though the blameworthy personnel have departed. How can the dependency thesis account for such blame?

Consider the Hooker Chemical Company, which had, for about six years prior to 1952, been dumping toxic wastes secretly and without permission into the ground of an area it owned, known as the Love Canal, near Niagara Falls, New York. Some years after it had stopped doing so, it gave up the Love Canal property, and houses were built on the site. By the late 1970s, people in the houses were experiencing foul odors and various debilitating symptoms, apparently caused by the seepage of the toxic chemicals into their basements. By the time this was discovered, all the personnel at Hooker responsible for the dumping had long since left the company. But the residents of the area blamed the company for their plight, and sued for damages.[1]

Of interest here are not the legal questions, but three others related to the moral issues. First is the question of whether the residents, in attributing blame to the company, intended to attribute blame of a typically moral kind. Second is the question of whether and why their moral claim may have been well substantiated. Third is the question of whether the dependency thesis is consistent with the answers to the first two, and thus whether one may blame the company although none of its present personnel are to blame. There is strong support for an affirmative answer to all three.

Given the full horror of the fate that befell the residents, it seems clear that in blaming the company, they meant to attribute blame in its most serious and far-reaching senses. By attributing moral blame, they likely sought to justify their pursuit of legal damages. The outcome of this pursuit would then in turn further establish the moral blameworthiness of the company and their moral rights to the damages won through legal means.

The evidence that the company is to blame includes a number of considerations. One is that company personnel in the line of duty dumped the toxic waste and should have known it could be hazardous to the environment and to people. A second is that employees Hooker assigned to give the land to the local board of education had access to records on its past use, should have checked them, and should have released specific information about potential hazards.[2] The failure to do these things was a dereliction of moral duty, whether or not they were committed by company employees working before the era of public environmental consciousness. The important points here are that company personnel had moral duties, should have known this, violated these duties, and these violations took part as a result of their employment by Hooker Chemical. Moreover, whether or not the residents knew of any specific Hooker employees who might be to blame, they had evidence that some such employees had been involved, and evidence that they were to blame because of the nature of their relationship to Hooker.

In blaming Hooker Chemical, the residents of Love Canal were apparently attributing blame to a company for its past practices, even though these practices were carried on by personnel who had long since left the company. There is no clear evidence that the residents were attributing blame only to the Hooker Chemical Company of the past. Whether or not they had good reason to blame the present Hooker Chemical is another matter. Regardless of this question, they did attribute blame to it, and appear to have meant what they said. Indeed, such attributions are not particularly uncommon in our moral lives. Now, for example, a half century later, many Serbians blame Croatia, its people, leaders, and government for siding with the Nazis in World War II and then persecuting and massacring Serbian populations. However uncharitable they may be, however they may promote further conflicts, such attributions do appear to make some sense, even if ultimately, upon careful scrutiny, the evidence supporting them is contentious.

The dependency thesis does not deny the possibility of presently blaming an organization for past practice although the blameworthy individuals have, by now, left. Dependency requires that in order for an organization to be blameworthy, some of its personnel must be, as well. It does not require these to be present personnel in the firm. Nor does it require them to be alive at the present time. Dependency requires that some people, who are or were personnel in the company, must be to blame for violating their duties to take steps to prevent the morally objectionable matter from occurring. It requires that in order to blame the organization, one must have evidence that some of its personnel, whether past or present, share in some blame for contributing to the morally objectionable matter at hand.

Dependency is not based on, nor does it imply any metaphysical connection between the blameworthiness of the two. That is, it does not imply that an organization is in fact morally blameworthy because in it lie some blameworthy people. There is no implication here that the blameworthiness of the personnel somehow makes the organization blameworthy or taints it, or that their blameworthiness is like a disease, spreading out from the personnel to infect the whole. There is no question here, implied by dependency, of whether or not the personnel are still in the organization, still tainting it with their guilt. Dependency asserts simply that whether or not the blameworthy individuals are still present, a necessary condition for plausibly blaming the organization is that there be, in a temporally indefinite sense, such individuals, and that one have some evidence of this at the time of blaming. That the residents of Love Canal have such evidence is clear, and so the dependency thesis allows the possibility of their blaming Hooker Chemical.

Now whether or not their blaming Hooker Chemical is really a rational thing to do given the extent of the change it has undergone is quite another matter. The dependency thesis does not offer any clear insight on this question. There are many considerations which one may bring to bear on both sides of the issue. But these are separate from the dependency thesis.

Such questions have much in common with those that arise when one blames an individual for something. Is one saying that the individual or the organization is now blameworthy for something done in the past? If so, what if each had undergone profound changes since the morally objectionable act was committed? What if the individual had a total change of character, had become "born again," or had a brain transplant? What if all the personnel in the organization had changed, the relevant policies and procedures had changed, and there were now new safeguards to prevent the kinds of abuses experienced in the past?  The changes may be, perhaps, sufficient to show that the blame is presently pointless.  Jean-Paul Sartre might, of course disagree, holding that once one has done wrong, one has done it and is blameworthy for doing so into eternity.  But there is no need to enter such moral and metaphysical disputes at this point.  Dependency does not take clear sides on them.  They may be settled by an honest assessment of a wide variety of considerations favoring each viewpoint.  Dependency is merely a necessary condition for plausibly attributing moral blame.

## 3.2 Blaming An Organization When Its Personnel Did Their Jobs

There may appear to be an inverse relationship between organizational blameworthiness and the degree to which one has performed according to the duties of one's role or position in an organization.  Consider a situation in which some untoward thing has happened in the context of one's work, one failed to prevent it, but, on moral grounds, one could and should have.  Whether or not one's neglect accorded with one's prescribed duties may affect the plausibility of a claim that the organization is to blame for the untoward event.

If one's official duties did not require the neglect in question, the blame for the matter likely will be heaped on the individual alone.  There may be no temptation to try to blame the organization, since the individual's neglect resulted from that individual acting on one's own.  If, on the other hand, the neglect resulted from one's clearly prescribed duties and one's actions as a faithful employee of some organization, there may be some reason to blame the organization, regardless of whether or not the individual is exonerated.  For now the policies of the organization may be perceived as playing an important causal role in the untoward matter.

The important question here is whether the analysis of chapters one and two in fact contradicts such distinctions.  It does not matter for the plausibility of that analysis whether or not it provides grounds to draw the present distinction.  Its purpose is not to draw all distinctions relevant to all questions of organizational blame.  But it should be consistent with many such distinctions which are commonly drawn in regard to such questions.  That is, such commonly drawn distinctions should not offer reason to doubt the analysis.

Consider the case in which the neglect resulted from the employee faithfully carrying out the prescribed duties of the job, just as the employer has directed.  Why might one be tempted to consider blaming the employer?  The obvious reason is that the duties prescribed by the employer are viewed as deficient.  They should have been different than they were.  To say that they should have been different is to say that it is morally objectionable that they in fact were not.  To have evidence that it was morally objectionable to the point justifying an attribution of blame requires evidence, as argued in 2.2 and 2.3, that someone in the organization, who could have corrected the matter, should have known and taken steps. Whether or not we have evidence of who such individuals are, and whether or not there are in fact any such specific individuals, the fact is that someone should have known. For if it is not true that someone should have known and acted, then, as argued in 2.2 and 2.3, blaming the organization is vacuous. So, to assert plausibly that the organization is to blame requires that we have evidence that someone should have known and acted, whether or not this evidence points to any specific individuals. In conclusion, if some organizational policy is morally deficient to an extent which warrants blaming the organization, the extent to which evidence of this reveals evidence of individual moral deficiency is the extent to which the organizational moral deficiency is consistent with the dependency thesis and the five conditions.

Suppose, on the other hand, that the known moral deficiency of some policy violates the sufficiency thesis, and we know exactly which superiors are to blame and to what extent for misdirecting the employee. We may then attribute blame to each of them appropriately. Would there, then, be any purpose to attribute blame to the organization? Of course, there may be utilitarian, legal, or political reasons to penalize the organization. However, as argued in 1.5, to justify such penalties, one need not attribute blame to the organization. Furthermore, the significant purposes of blaming can best be satisfied by blaming the responsible persons individually.

If an individual is known to have strayed from the duties of one's job, then the individual may be blamed, and no significant purpose is best served by blaming the organization. If the individual is blameworthy because the requirements of the job were being followed, then either someone in the organization is to blame for those requirements, or none are. If it is known that absolutely none are, then the individual truly was a victim of circumstances, and there is no present basis for attributing moral blame to anyone or any organization at all. If there is some reason to believe that others are to blame, but it is not clear exactly who is or just to what extent they are, then one may choose to blame the organization, given evidence that part of what makes them blameworthy is their involvement in the organization.

The analysis of chapters one and two certainly allows the possibility of establishing a relationship between the inclination to blame an organization and the question of whether its personnel followed their duties. But this analysis does not take sides on the issue. Whether one can establish such a relationship is a matter which is logically independent of the analysis, and is to be decided on independent grounds. Such a relationship would have no bearing on the five conditions for making attributions of organizational moral blame.

### 3.3 Blaming an Organization Because Its Personnel Are Not to Blame

It appears in some cases that the very lack of a human cause may lead people to consider blaming the organization. If so, however, there may be another possible problem for the thesis of individual dependency. According to this thesis, for an organization to be blameworthy, some of its personnel must also be to blame for their contribution, and there must be evidence that some do. If, on the other hand, we are motivated to blame the organization because we lack such evidence, organizational blameworthiness would appear to have no relationship to the blameworthiness of personnel.

Consider the following scenario. Several computer enthusiasts band together to form a small company selling a small but user-friendly computer that they manufacture, at first, in the garage of one of their members. After a few months, they move into a few rooms of an old building downtown that they rent at a rather low rate. The firm grows rapidly during the early part of its second year, expanding to take over the building in which it is located. All the partners work very hard, and the computer is a smashing success, bringing them profits beyond their wildest dreams. Enamored with their success, the partners and their families buy large houses, new furnishings, new cars and other luxuries, plunging themselves into debt far beyond their present incomes.

All goes well until the middle of the second year, when their building burns down. This is no small disaster, as it turns out, since, first of all, they had no fire insurance. Second, they had in the building much technical information that was not stored elsewhere and could be duplicated later only at very great expense. Third, their incomes plummeted so severely that their families had most of their luxuries repossessed.

Now imagine the perspective of the spouses of the partners, dismayed at the loss of their luxuries. They might very well attribute blame in a typically moral sense to their spouses and the other partners. They might say that the partners were irresponsible in allowing them to buy the luxuries. They might go on to argue that the partners should have been more careful in their business dealings, taking out insurance, and making sure all technical information was carefully protected from fire and theft.

The partners may well have some rather reasonable responses to the anger of their spouses. They may each individually deny blameworthiness for their lax business procedures. That is, each may offer convincing reasons why it was not the duty of that one to think about taking out fire insurance and protecting the technical information. One of the partners might have been solely involved in marketing, one in arranging production, another in technical design, and so forth. And each may well have been extremely busy and over-worked. Indeed, it may well be the strong commitment of each to his or her appropriate roles that had led the company to its early and dramatic financial successes. So it may seem plausible, to each of the partners, that none of them had time or energy to consider, discuss, or address within the firm such matters as office management, security, or insurance.

Despite all this, the spouses may insist that it was indeed someone's responsibility to think of such things and bring them forth for a decision. So, it might appear that the spouses accept the exculpatory excuse of each partner individually, yet still blame their organization for the loss. And their viewpoint is not unreasonable. After all, the loss did not result solely from the blind forces of nature, as the fire may have. The loss could well have been avoided by some more prudent policies of the firm. It may be precisely because the spouses accept the excuses of each partner that they attribute blame to the firm. The problem here is that the spouses' viewpoint appears reasonable, and also appears to contradict the dependency thesis. And the question is whether this presents a genuine exception to that thesis. That it does not can be understood through consideration of that thesis.

The dependency thesis does not state that in order for an organization to be blameworthy, there must be evidence of at least one particular named person in it who is in fact partially to blame for the matter at hand. To blame an organization, we need not actually have an individual culprit in focus. All we need is evidence that, in general, there must be someone who deserves some blame for contributing to the matter. That is, there must be some evidence at hand that supports the likelihood that some of the personnel in the organization deserve some blame for the matter. If there is no evidence that there are any who do, then, as explained in 2.2, there would be a lack of evidence that the organization could reasonably be expected to have done anything to prevent the matter at hand. Blaming the organization would be more like blaming a machine than like blaming its operator.

Organizations are said to act when their personnel perform organizational duties and practices. What is described as an organizational duty is a duty for its personnel to carry out. But if none of them have any such duty, or if none of them could carry out such duties, then the evidence supporting a statement that an organization has a duty is no different from that supporting the statement that a machine has a duty. Yet, that is largely an elliptical way of speaking. To assert that an organization has a duty is supported by evidence that those in it should perform as if it does. That is, to support the claim that an organization has a moral duty requires evidence that if some of its personnel do not perform in certain appropriate ways, they deserve blame for shirking one or more of their moral duties. The evidence supporting a claim that an organization has a duty supports the duty of its personnel to see that the outcome of their performances can be appropriately described as the fulfillment of the organizations's duty.

Now the computer spouses do not have evidence firmly supporting just which individuals in the firm are guilty of dereliction of duty or to what extent. The exculpatory excuses of the partners apparently succeed in foiling the attempts to locate the exact individuals and clarify the degree of blameworthiness of each. But the spouses do have evidence that there was a duty that someone in the firm should have carried out. Such evidence may include the following: it is normal business practice to plan for fire; knowledge of this was available to all the partners; there is a general duty of married people to take precautions to protect their families from financial risk, etc. So the spouses have evidence that there must be some individual partners in the firm who failed in their duties, although it is unclear just which ones did, and to what extent. In possessing such evidence, the spouses, in blaming the organization, do not contradict the dependency thesis.

To say that the spouses have such evidence does not require that one side with them in their dispute with the partners. It is doubtful that sufficient information has been given in this brief sketch of the case to give firm support to a conclusion about who has the stronger argument. After all, it is at least imaginable that each individual partner has such a strong exculpatory excuse that the charge that none of them are to blame is plausible. Perhaps, on balance, the firm is not really to blame at all, and the loss was simply an occurrence of bad luck that no human beings could possibly have prevented without having sacrificed the early success of the firm. That is, perhaps it was true that if any of the partners had been more concerned with insurance and security, they would have lacked the time and energy to be so successful. Perhaps they had to take the risk they did, and were simply unlucky. Perhaps, that is, neither the firm nor any personnel can be shown to be blameworthy.

From the perspective of the spouses, this latter conclusion seems rather far-fetched. If the partners could establish this case, the spouses would likely retort that the partners should have at least told the spouses that there was no insurance on the building and technical information. If they should have, then there is reason to think that some people are blameworthy, and evidence to support either the claim that the firm is to blame, or some of its partners are to blame, or both.

It is important to understand that the analysis of chapters one and two does not aspire to provide an easy means of resolving such disputes as the one between the partners and their spouses. The dispute must be settled in the way that such disputes are normally addressed. One would examine many more considerations and details to try to pinpoint the onus. And such efforts may or may not lead to a clear conclusion.

The important point here is that the position of the spouses does not contradict the dependency thesis. They do possess evidence that blame is attributable to someone in the firm. They may be motivated to blame the firm from their lack of certainty on just who in the firm is to blame. But since they have evidence that someone in it is to blame, they cannot be motivated to blame the firm by the lack of such evidence.

Suppose, on the other hand, that they are motivated to blame the firm by the belief, however mistaken it may be, that there is no evidence that any individuals at all share in any of the blame. The question is whether their blaming the firm, given only their belief, can be plausible. The dependency thesis maintains that there can be no good reason to blame an organization unless one has evidence that there must be someone in it to blame. Any attempt to blame an organization without such evidence must assume that a mechanism, a structure quite apart from all moral humans, can be a subject of moral blame. However, as argued in 2.2 and 2.3, such an assumption is inexplicable. To assert that an organization can have a duty although none of its personnel have any contributory duties is to stretch the meaning of "moral duty" beyond plausible limits. If organizations have duties, their personnel have contributory duties.

## 3.4 Blaming an Organization Without Blaming Its Personnel

Consideration of the spouses' view suggests a further objection to the dependency thesis quite apart from questions of evidence. This is the objection, consistent with the view of Peter French, that it is logically possible that an organization might be to blame although none of its personnel share in any of that blame at all. It appears that one may say such a thing, and that doing so is not inconsistent. One may, after all, intend that it is simply two different things for an organization to be blameworthy and for some of its personnel to be blameworthy. One may intend that the blameworthiness of an organization does not require that any of its personnel are in any way blameworthy for their parts in the matter.

It is important to understand that the dependency thesis does not deny the logical point that such a statement with such intended meaning can be made. There may well be no logical contradiction in making it, and some people may actually make such statements, intending to separate the blameworthiness of an organization entirely from that of its personnel. However, the argument for the dependency thesis advances serious objections to making or intending such a statement.

The problem with holding that the blameworthiness of an organization is independent of the blameworthiness of its personnel is that it is pragmatically incoherent. That is, it does not advance the main purposes of moral discourse. Rather, it ignores such purposes in order to make a statement that sounds plausible, but that is, within our moral life, vacuous.

The purposes of blaming an organization are primarily to attribute moral guilt, justify punishment, and to indicate to intelligent moral agents some ways in which practices must be changed in order to avoid moral blameworthiness. If organizations are morally blameworthy independently of their personnel, then their personnel need not feel any moral compunction about the performance described as that of the organization. For in that case, it may well be that no personnel have performed in blameworthy ways. Therefore, the statement that the organization is to blame has no moral implications for humans. It means simply that the organization has, unfortunately, acted immorally; but we personnel need not feel badly, and need have no moral compunction about this. It is not our fault, in any moral sense, that the organization is to blame. It is at worst a bit of bad luck, that we might or might not choose to address in our work, depending on other considerations. But this question is separate from the question of the moral blameworthiness of the organization.

There is, therefore, a significant loss of meaning in a statement of organizational blame that is intended to make no reflection on the blameworthiness of its personnel. For such a statement is powerless to do what such statements normally accomplish: to attribute blame, justify punishment, or convey beliefs about what moral practice is. To assert that it is logically possible to make such a statement is, then, an idle point, of little or no significance for normal moral purposes and discourse.

None of this denies that the spouses of the computer firm partners may in fact mean by blaming the firm that none of the partners deserve any moral blame. Furthermore, they may even have reasons for meaning this. Perhaps they wish to express their strong feelings without insulting the partners, their spouses, and without worsening their marriages. Perhaps they want to express their displeasure in a subtle way, which suggests gently to the partners the need for more care in such matters in the future. But if this is what they mean, they are depriving their words of the power of moral blame. By exonerating the partners of such blame, their statements in fact lack moral force.

According to the dependency thesis, the essential moral force of statements of organizational blame requires that some individuals of the organization are at least partially to blame for contributing to the untoward matter at hand. The plausibility of such statements requires, furthermore, the presence of some evidence that some of the personnel of the organization are at least partially to blame. The logical possibility that one could blame an organization without implicating any of its personnel is not a significant objection to this thesis. It is formulated to capture the import of organizational blame in contexts where such blame has its full and usual moral force. By basing his theory on the logical point, separating organizational and human blameworthiness, French has ignored essential pragmatic dimensions of moral language and discourse.

### 3.5 The Argument for Dependency and the Sea of Green Fallacy

The argument establishing the thesis of individual dependency proceeded from two questions. First was the question of whether an organization could be blameworthy if none of its personnel were in any way blameworthy for the matter at hand. Second was the question of whether one could have good reason to blame an organization if one had no evidence that any of its personnel were in any way blameworthy for the matter at hand. It was found that any alleged blameworthiness of an organization is inexplicable if in fact none of its personnel are in any way blameworthy. Moreover, a total lack of evidence of individual blameworthiness deprives one of conclusive evidence that the organization is to blame. It was concluded that for an organization to be blameworthy, some of its personnel must share in that blame and in order to support the claim of organizational blameworthiness, one must have some evidence that some of its personnel are to blame as well.

Now one might object to the logic of this argument on the grounds that it is based on a version of the Fallacy of Subtraction, which will be described here as the "sea of green fallacy." Imagine a football game at which each fan at one end of the stadium holds up, during half time, at a given prompt, a one-foot-square piece of colored cardboard. Watching the football game on television, one notices that this phenomenon creates a visual impression of green covering those fans. Later, however, the announcers interview some of the organizers of the visual phenomenon, who explain that what actually happened was different from what appearances indicate. Actually, every other fan held up a blue-colored cardboard, and the alternate fans a yellow one. What was actually a checkerboard square of blue and yellow appeared to television audiences, from a distance, to be a solid green.

The fallacy occurred in the statement of the organizers, when they were discussing the display. One of them said, "If you take away the blue or yellow cardboards, there would be no green at all. In fact, you could say that in reality, there is no green at all, just blue and yellow." It is clearly a mistake to think that removal of the blue and yellow cards, and thus removal of the basis of the green, proves that there was no green, but only blue and yellow.

And likewise, one may argue, the argument for the dependency thesis is based on the sea of green fallacy. For it is a mistake to think that removal of all the blameworthy individuals, and thus removal of the basis for attributing organizational blame, proves that the organization was not to blame, but that only individuals were to blame. Just as the viewers did in fact see a sea of green in the stands, one may argue, the organization really is to blame. This blame, moreover, is quite a different matter from questions of whether or not the individuals are to blame. When the spouses blame the partners in the computer firm for the disaster, or the residents of Love Canal blame Hooker Chemical, they are blaming these organizations quite irrespective of whether or not their personnel are to blame. The argument for the dependency thesis appears to ignore the actual intended meanings of intelligent speakers of the language who earnestly and thoughtfully attribute moral blame to organizations.

The objection, however, is based on two subtle misconstruals of the argument for the dependency thesis. First, that argument does not establish any thesis about the meaning of attributions of organizational blame. It does not conclude anything about what the residents or the spouses really mean by attributing blame. Dependency allows them to mean what they wish, regardless of whether or not they have good evidence for their views. Dependency asserts that if they have good evidence supporting an ordinary, moral meaning of their views, and thus supporting moral purposes, this will include evidence that some personnel are also at least partly to blame for the matter at hand. Dependency is a thesis stating a necessary condition for making a plausible and well-supported claim of organizational blame.

The objection concludes its interpretation of the analogical argument for dependency with the claim that only individuals are to blame. This, however, is not a conclusion of the argument for dependency. That argument does not conclude that organizations are not to blame, nor that only individuals are. It concludes that individual blameworthiness is a necessary condition for organizational blameworthiness. The conclusion of that argument is that there may be evidence to support the blaming of organizations, that one may make statements attributing blame to organizations, and that such statements may have more or less evidence in support of them.

Second, the objection misconstrues the similarities and differences between the sea of green fallacy and the argument for dependency. That latter is directed to identify a necessary condition for attributing, plausibly and to accomplish ordinary moral purposes, organizational blame. It is no fallacy, in establishing such a condition, to ask if the blame is plausible in the absence of some evidence or putative condition. The argument shows that in the absence of individual blameworthiness and any evidence of it, organizational blame is groundless.

The sea of green fallacy is a fallacy precisely because it does not establish a necessary condition for the sea of green. The blue and yellow cards are not necessary conditions for the television viewers to experience the sea of green. The fans in the stands could have held up green cards producing the same visual impression to television viewers. The fallacious statement of the organizers concludes that there does not in fact exist any real green because it is possible to take away blue cards and yellow cards and then have nothing we would be inclined to describe as green. But the argument for dependency does not conclude that organizational blame does not exist because it is possible to take away all individual blame and then have no grounds to attribute organizational blame. It argues, rather, that organizational blame requires evidence of individual blameworthiness. If, on the other hand, the organizer of the sea of green had said that, "The television viewers' experience of green depended upon the fans holding up blue and yellow cards," this person would have committed no fallacy. The blue and yellow cards did, in fact, cause the television sensation of green, and the viewers' experience at that time did depend in this causal sense on the showing of these cards. But the argument for dependency does not establish that individual blameworthiness causes organizational blameworthiness. It establishes only that individual blameworthiness is a logically necessary condition for blaming an organization.

## 3.6 Chapter Summary

The chapter addresses several problematic cases and questions pertaining to the dependency thesis and the proposed necessary and sufficient conditions for making plausible attributions of organizational blame. The limited nature of these proposals serves as the main basis for their defense. The fact that they do not commit one to specification of a single, proper meaning of attributions of organizational blame is a major source of their strength.

The first section addresses the question of whether the dependency thesis allows one to blame an organization even if it is known that all of its blameworthy personnel have departed. Whether there is good reason to blame an organization under such circumstances is a debatable matter requiring much further inquiry. Of present importance is simply the fact that dependency allows such a possibility and again, does not take sides on this issue.

Second is the question of whether or not organizations are more likely to be blameworthy if employees were following orders. The five conditions for blaming put forth in chapter two certainly allow one to make such a case. Whether or not one can, however, is another matter, irrelevant to the adequacy of the five.

The third section addresses the problem posed by cases in which it is the very lack of known blameworthy individuals that leads one to blame the organization. This apparent violation of dependency turned out to be illusory. Virtually any information that is complete enough to establish that an organization is to blame in the full, moral sense is bound to include evidence that some individuals are as well, even if their specific identities are unclear.

Fourth is an apparent problem for dependency according to which people may intend, in blaming an organization, to blame none of its individuals. It was pointed out that dependency does not prohibit such intentions. It indicates, however, that such blame will be lacking in typical moral force. Dependency maintains that if evidence of individual blameworthiness is entirely lacking, statements blaming an organization cannot fulfill the important purposes of such blame, such as those described in 1.5 and 1.6. However, the five conditions allow that different speakers of the language may, in blaming an organization, have a wide range of different intended meanings. How this may be so, and what meanings may be allowed is taken up in the next chapter.

The fifth section addresses an attack on the logic of the argument for the dependency thesis. This attack was shown to be based on two misconceptions of that argument. First, that argument does not purport to prove that claims of organizational blame in fact blame individuals. Second, the attack is based on an analogy that is irrelevant because, unlike the argument for dependency, the argument in the analogy does not seek to establish a necessary condition.

The exploration of these issues clarifies the limited nature of the analysis of chapters one and two. That analysis is directed to establish conditions of plausible assertibility, not conditions of truth. Such conditions may, of course, be used as the basis for speculation about the meaning of such attributions. The latter part of 2.5 and also 2.6 contain such speculation, which is consistent with the eighth purpose of blaming organizations noted in 1.6. Of special importance here is the fact that the analysis of chapters one and two is not directed to state a single, true meaning of claims of organizational blame.

The approach taken here should not, however, be interpreted to imply that it is particularly inappropriate or problematic to speculate about the meaning of claims of organizational blame. Indeed, such speculations are developed further in chapters four and seven. However, such speculations are better developed after analyses of purpose and evidence are clearly established. These analyses should serve as a basis for such speculations, not as offshoots of a prior commitment to a theory of what people do or must mean by their words.

**Notes**

1. Donald G. McNeil, Jr., "Health Chief Calls Waste Site a 'Peril'," *The New York Times*, 3 August 1978, 1, 18.

2. *Ibid.*

# Chapter 4

## Distribution, Meaning, and Evidence

The first three chapters establish and clarify a set of conditions specifying the range of evidence that may confirm an attribution of moral blame to an organization. These conditions require that when an organization is blamed, some but not all of the individuals within it must be to blame for their parts in the blameworthy matter at hand. The present chapter is directed to clarify the implications of these conditions and this requirement in regard to questions of the distribution of blame within an organization.

The five conditions do not specify exactly what, within a given organization, makes it blameworthy. Instead, they state conditions under which one might plausibly attribute moral blameworthiness to the organization. In requiring that one have evidence that some but not all of the individuals within the organization share some blame for contributing to the blameworthy matter at hand, they may appear to imply that blaming an organization distributes some blame to some but not all of its personnel. This, however, is not an implication of the five conditions.

The five are conditions of warranted assertibility, not clarifications of the meaning of claims of organizational blameworthiness. They do not indicate a single coherent meaning which one must have in asserting that an organization is to blame. They do not constitute a metaphysical theory of that in which organizational blameworthiness consists. They are not committed to a theory of just what organizational blameworthiness is. They do not isolate some state or property that is unique to blameworthy organizations, and lacking in those that are not blameworthy. Nor do they answer all questions about the relationship of organizational blameworthiness to individual blameworthiness. Finally, neither do they imply any particular view about the distribution of blame within an organization which is judged morally blameworthy.

This last point can be perhaps most clearly established by examining the compatibility of a statement of organizational blame and another statement about the distribution of that blame. The five conditions are compatible with several alternate construals of distributivity. The reasons for this compatibility further clarify the limitations and significance of these conditions.

There are four possible ways in which a statement of organizational blameworthiness may distribute blame. It may distribute blame to all the individuals in the organization, to some specifically identified individuals within it, to some indefinite group of individuals within it, or to no individuals within it. None of these construals are ruled out as meaningless or incoherent by the five conditions.

### 4.1 Are All the Personnel to Blame?

The first possibility, which may be referred to as the distributivity thesis, is that in blaming an organization, one may intend that all of its personnel are to blame. There can be little doubt that sometimes, in blaming an organization, some people may indeed intend to be blaming all of the individuals in the organization. Such an intended meaning is clearly coherent, and could be supported by available evidence. But is it consistent with the thesis of individual sufficiency? Distributivity appears to assert that all the individuals in the organization are to blame, and sufficiency appears to require that not all are. In fact, however, the apparent contradiction is illusory.

To intend to distribute blame to all the individuals in an organization does not require that one have total, complete evidence establishing the exact degree of blame of every blameworthy individual. To distribute blame to all the individuals in the organization does not necessarily mean that one has distributed all the blame to all these individuals, and that no blame is left over. Rather, it means at least that some indefinite share of blame is distributed to each individual. Moreover, one may meaningfully blame all the individuals in the organization even though one does not have conclusive evidence that all are in fact to blame. So, of course, one may intend to blame all the individuals in the organization even though one does not know the nature or degree of the blameworthiness of all the individuals who are blameworthy for the untoward matter at hand.

These points distinguish the sufficiency thesis from the distributivity thesis. Sufficiency states that there is no significant moral purpose to blaming an organization when there is complete knowledge of the blameworthiness of every blameworthy individual. Distributivity asserts that one may intend, in blaming an organization, to be blaming all individuals within it. Sufficiency is a thesis about the significance of blaming under conditions of complete knowledge of individual blameworthiness. Distributivity is a thesis about the intended distribution of blame to individuals within an organization when making a claim of organizational blame.

Consider the possibility of a case that is consistent with distributivity, but appears to contradict sufficiency. Suppose that in blaming an organization, one intends to be laying blame on all of its personnel. Suppose that, in addition, one also has complete knowledge of the degree of blameworthiness of all blameworthy personnel, and that this list includes all the personnel of the organization. Does the sufficiency thesis forbid one from blaming the organization? It is important to understand that it does not.

Sufficiency points out that in blaming the organization under such conditions, one's doing so is morally superfluous. The significant moral purposes can be fulfilled by blaming the individuals. To say, "All these people are blameworthy" is more accurate and morally efficacious than saying, "The organization is blameworthy." However, people can and do utter statements whose purposes can be fulfilled, and even better fulfilled, by other statements. The intended meaning of a statement is one thing, while its usefulness, value or purpose may be quite another. To the extent that the five conditions of section 2.5 are not conditions of meaningfulness, they allow the possibility that a claim of organizational blame may be distributive.

The five conditions do not state necessary and sufficient conditions under which a claim of organizational blame is meaningful in all respects, nor do they dictate what the meaning of such a claim must be. They are pragmatic conditions--that is, they cite conditions under which such claims may serve ordinary moral purposes. They need not be viewed as restricting one to any one particular purpose, or as requiring speakers of the language to conform to such a purpose. Their importance is that (1) people do often attribute organizational blame under such circumstances; (2) certain intelligible moral purposes may be served by attributing it under them; (3) there are no significant additional moral purposes to be served by attributing it in violation of these conditions; and (4) attributing it in violation of these conditions fails to serve certain moral purposes as well as attributions which do not violate them.

This last condition is particularly important. The argument in 1.5 supported the view that, given complete evidence of individual blameworthiness, it is actually preferable to blame individuals instead of the organization. It is preferable because doing so captures more accurately the significance of the evidence one possesses. If one knows all the individuals who are responsible and the extent of the blameworthiness of each, one actually has more specific information than that conveyed in the claim, "The organization is to blame." One can now address the blameworthiness of each individual in an entirely appropriate manner. To blame the organization instead of the individuals in such cases is to mask the exact blameworthiness of each individual.

However, it is still true that the five conditions do not condemn, as meaningless, attributions of organizational blame which are based on different evidence, and directed to further different purposes. The conditions simply indicate that these other attributions are not maximally efficacious in a typically moral sense.

Is there, then, any good reason why one might choose to blame an organization, if in dong so one intended to blame all its personnel, and one had conclusive evidence of the precise degree of blameworthiness of each? That is, why not simply blame the individuals and clarify the blame deserved by each? A number of answers are possible here. First, one may name the organization instead of the individuals simply because it is easier to do so. Second, one may do so under the impression that blaming the organization and blaming all its personnel amount to the same thing. Third, one may do so in the belief that blaming the organization is a more effective way of calling attention to the significance of organizational roles and interconnections than blaming the individuals.

These three purposes are, however, weak. None of them offers compelling reason to blame the organization instead of the individuals who are known to be blameworthy. No significant purposes are served which may not be better served by blaming the individuals and clarifying the ways and extent to which they are blameworthy. Although it is not meaningless to blame the organization instead of the personnel in such cases, it is not morally advantageous to do so.

In conclusion, the five conditions do not prove that one may not intend, in attributing blame to an organization, to blame all of its personnel. They indicate that if one has too much evidence, it is weak and ineffectual to do so. But this is a disadvantage resulting in part from the quantity of evidence one has, not from one's intention to distribute blame alone. The five conditions do not attribute meaninglessness to attributions in such situations.

## 4.2 Are Some but not All the Personnel to Blame?

The second possible interpretation of the distribution of a claim of organizational blame is that in making the claim, one distributes the blame to some but not all of the personnel in the organization. This may be referred to as the "nondistributive" option. There are two main ways of construing this option. First is the possibility that in blaming the organization, blame is being distributed to some indefinite group of individuals within the organizational framework. Second is the possibility that one is attributing blame to some specific individuals within the organizational framework. It is worth noting here that Larry May's theory of vicarious negligence may be interpreted along either line. And each may be consistent with the five conditions.

Consider first the possibility that the blame is distributed to some indefinite group of personnel within the organizational structure. It should be clear at this point that the five conditions certainly allow this to be the intended reference of organizational blame. Indeed, these conditions suggest, although they do not require or entail, that this is a fitting interpretation of the meaning of a claim of organizational blame.

The dependency thesis states that an organization cannot be blameworthy unless some of its individuals are and that one cannot have grounds to assert such blame unless one has evidence that some individuals are. Again, however, one need not have evidence that any particular individuals are blameworthy. Therefore, it is entirely possible that the individual blameworthiness of an indefinite number of organizational personnel is at the heart of an attribution of organizational blameworthiness.

If one holds that it is, one can explain the purpose of attributing blame to the organization instead of the individuals in the following way. One does so because one is not sure of all the people in the organization who are blameworthy, or to what extent. But one has some evidence that some are, and evidence that their blameworthiness likely arose in the context and perhaps as a result of their organizational interconnections and roles. So, in response to the limited evidence available, one blames the organization rather than stating, somewhat blandly, "Some people in that organization are probably to blame due to their roles and involvement in the organization." By blaming the organization, one calls attention to the need to investigate the blameworthiness of individuals in the context of their organizational roles and interrelationships. In doing so, one may very well intend to distribute blame to some individuals in the organization without intending to blame any particular individuals which one has identified.

Consider here Larry May's construal of corporate vicarious responsibility. His work suggests that a corporation may be vicariously blameworthy for the negligence of one or more of its personnel if that negligence resulted from a corporate grant of authority, and some members of the corporation could and should have taken effective preventive measures.[1] As discussed in 6.5, such a construal is also consistent with the five conditions.

If, in attributing corporate blame, one intends to attribute vicarious negligence to some individuals, to whom is one distributing this blame: to an indefinite number of personnel in the organization, or to some specifically named or identified individuals? The five conditions allow either answer. One may be referring to an indefinite number for the very same reasons as explained above. Or one may be referring to some identified or unidentified specific individuals if one thinks they are the culprits, they are part of the organization, and that their organizational roles and interconnections offer an important part of the explanation of their blameworthiness.

The second interpretation of the nondistributive construal is that in attributing blame to an organization, one may attribute blame to some specific set of individuals who lie within the organizational network but do not exhaust the list of corporate personnel. That is, one may have in mind a list of individuals who one believes are each individually blameworthy, and, in attributing blame to the organization, actually intend to blame only the individuals on that list.

Such a construal need not contradict the import of the five conditions. Because they are merely conditions of evidence, they allow a number of intended meanings. But why would one bother to blame the organization if one intended to blame merely some of its personnel? Suppose that one intended to direct all one's blame to these personnel. Then why not do so instead of blaming the organization? In light of the five conditions, one might respond that one does not yet have conclusive evidence of all the personnel who are to blame or of their exact degree of blameworthiness. Thus, one may be hedging one's bets. One names the organization in the belief that further inquiry will show that even if one's list is inadequate for some reason, the rest of the blameworthy individuals will likely turn out to be connected through the organizational structure.

## 4.3 Are None of the Personnel to Blame?

The third interpretation of questions of the distribution of blame within an organization is that in blaming an organization, one does not attribute blame to any of the individuals in the organization. Could one, in blaming the organization, be blaming no individuals whatever? Once again, because the five are conditions of evidence, not meaningfulness, they permit one to have such intentions.

Why would one choose to blame an organization while intending to blame none of its personnel? Various motives for such intent are readily imagined. One might lack clear evidence of individual wrongdoing and choose to blame a corporation and avoid blaming its personnel. Wanting to avoid the divisive consequences of attributing blame to one's spouse, one of the spouses of the computer firm partners discussed in 3.3 might blame the firm while insisting that the blame was not directed at any of the individual partners. Such considerations may well play important roles in people's lives, and induce one to blame an organization without distributing blame to any of its individual personnel.

If such considerations impel one to blame with such intentions, then what could be the meaning of such blame? What important moral purposes could it serve? It is in response to these questions that a weak version of the theory of corporate moral personhood may be helpful. French has made a plausible case that one can blame an organization intelligibly without distributing blame to its personnel. He has shown that one may intelligibly attribute blame without intending to distribute it within the organization to any of its personnel. He has argued that one may attribute blame to an organization and be interpreted coherently as distributing the blame to no one but the organization itself.

Such an interpretation is possible because one may coherently refer to an organization as a moral person.  There are, of course, differences between humans and organizations.  But there are also similarities, and these may be described by the term "moral personhood," as long as it is recognized that this is an abstract metaphysical concept whose meaning is explicated by a philosophical analysis such as that French develops.  French's concept of moral personhood is a carefully defined and clarified abstraction that establishes an important moral similarity between humans and organizations.  But it does not establish, and French does not take it to establish, that organizations are somehow on a par with humans in every moral respect.

What, then, does it mean to blame an organization if, in doing so, one is referring to it as a moral person?  It means that one is treating it as having certain important moral qualities which many humans also have.  It has the ability to deliberate and decide, and to acknowledge important duties to human beings.  Therefore, if it performs inappropriately, it should be blamed in a way similar to that in which we commonly blame humans with such abilities.[2]

French's work establishes the plausibility of one interpretation of an attribution of organizational blame.  But it does not establish, nor need it be viewed as establishing, the whole, single meaning of such attributions.  Neither does it establish the falsity of the dependency thesis or the sufficiency thesis.  Neither must we recognize it as having established the sharp ontological dichotomy which French claims for it, and the resultant dualistic theory criticized in chapter five.  As a theory of one possible intended meaning of a claim of organizational blame, however, part of French's work may be consistent with the analysis surrounding the five conditions.

## 4.4 Blaming an Organization as a Nondistributional Act

If the five conditions allow the above interpretations of how attributions of blame to an organization distribute the blame, do they allow the possibility that such attributions do not distribute blame at all?  It should be clear at this point that they do.  But what sense could it make to say "The organization is to blame," while acknowledging, at the same time, that one does not mean that, really, any one thing is to blame?

One might intend that such a statement does not attribute blame to anything at all if one disagreed with the position of Peter French, and maintained that there is no coherent, meaningful sense in which an organization can be a subject of moral predicates, a moral person, or literally blamed for anything.  Thus, one might, in a given case, detect no evidence of individual wrongdoing, and also find no sense in the idea that a corporation could meaningfully be blamed.  Yet, one might, at the same time, be moved by the potential significance of making a claim appearing to attribute blame to an organization.

That is, one might believe that such a claim could have an important and appropriate effect on other people. So one might make such a claim for rhetorical purposes.

If made for rhetorical purposes, what could such a claim, lacking any intended object, mean? It might be intended elliptically, as a kind of prediction. Although one does not attribute blame to anyone or to the organization as an entity, one uses the language of organizational blame to express one's belief that it may well turn out in the future that blame should be attributed, even if one does not now intend to attribute it to anyone or to an entity named "the organization." One intends the blame nonreferentially because one believes that one lacks sufficient evidence to support an attribution of blame to anything. One uses the language of blame, with a referential appearance, because one thinks that evidence to attribute blame will turn up in the future. Although such intent is logically possible, it is not clearly defensible, or likely to occur often.

It is important to understand why the five conditions do permit such an unusual interpretation. The fact that one possesses evidence of the presence of individual blameworthiness does not necessarily motivate one to want to blame individuals. One may think the available evidence makes it likely that blameworthiness will, in the future, be justifiably attributed. Yet one does not think this evidence supports the present attribution of blame to anyone or anything. One could attribute blame with no referential intent in the presence of rather weak evidence of individual blameworthiness.

It is an advantage of the five conditions that they do allow such a remote possibility. Their doing so is one measure of the variety and flexibility of language usage they allow and help one to understand. Their significance is not that of some rigid bifurcation of meaning or meaningfulness. Their value is rather as a tool to help one clarify people's thinking and assess its rationality in a given context.

## 4.5 The Five Conditions as Criteria of Meaning but not Distribution

The prior sections of this chapter explore the distributional meaning of attributions of organizational blame. The discussion indicates that the five conditions allow considerable latitude in the intended distributional meaning of this blame. They allow a plurality of possible meanings of such attributions, and thus a broad range of ordinary thought and language usage.

The openness of the five conditions regarding the distribution of blame raises a further question about the import of those conditions. Is there any respect in which they proscribe the meaning of attributions of organizational blame? Or are they, after all, completely irrelevant to all questions of meaning?

The answer is that the five conditions do have some limited but important implications for understanding the meaning of these attributions. They surely do not draw narrow boundaries within which that meaning must lie. But they do suggest the implausibility of certain possible intended meanings of such attributions.

It is important to recognize that a certain diversity of meaning must be allowed for by an analysis of any concept. Terms describing colors as well as terms describing moral attributes must be understood in light of a certain openness of meaning. The term "green" may apply to a range of different shades. One person may use the term to refer to one shade, while another uses it to refer to a different one. Similar points can be made about other nouns, adjectives, verbs, and adverbs, and also about organizational blameworthiness. Indeed, that is precisely the significance of the argument developed in the first four sections of this chapter. However, to allow some differences in intended meaning is not to endorse all possible meanings as morally significant.

The five conditions indicate that attributing blame to an organization does not best fulfill moral purposes if one either intends one's claim to mean any one or more of the following things, or if one believes that one or more of these are true:

~1. Whatever untoward matters occurred are those for which no human beings are morally to blame. For one reason or another, no one had a moral duty to take preventive measures.

~2. There is conclusive evidence of the exact degree of blameworthiness of all the people who are blameworthy for the matter in question.

~3. No one with any moral duty to prevent the matter at hand is related through the network of relevant organizational relationships.

~4. No one related through the organization who could possibly have been able to take preventive measures could, on reasonable moral grounds, have been expected to do so.

~5. If there was any dereliction of moral duty that resulted in the objectionable matter, it arose independently of all organizational roles and relationships of the relevant individuals.

Each of these directly contradicts one or more of the five conditions. So a statement attributing organizational blame together with any of these will not fulfill successfully the main purposes of moral blame.

There is a possible misinterpretation of the significance of ~1 through ~5 that must be carefully avoided. This stems from the possibility that one could, after all, state, "The organization is to blame," and then go on to indicate boldly that one meant by this or believed one or more of ~1 through ~5. There can in fact be little doubt that some people may be inclined to do this under certain circumstances and, for certain reasons, however trivial or indefensible they may be. But such intentions or beliefs do not reveal a weakness of the five conditions of warranted assertibility for blaming an organization. For it is unlikely that attributing blame to an organization could fulfill any of the ordinary purposes of blaming if such blame was coupled with intentions or beliefs including any of ~1 through ~5. That is, intentions or beliefs including ~1 through ~5 not only contradict the plausibility of the statement, "The organization is to blame," but deprive it of coherent purpose.

Consider, for example, one of the spouses of the partners of the computer firm of 3.3 who, distraught by the repossessions of their house and new Chevrolet Corvette, complains bitterly to friends about the blameworthiness of the firm for its lack of fire and disaster insurance. Word of this bitter blame then travels to the other spouse who is one of the partners in the firm, and who feels embarrassed by it. The partner now rebukes the spouse for this embarrassment. In doing so, the partner says:

"You have no right to blame me for the disaster."

"But I was not blaming you," replies the spouse.

"Your blaming the firm reflects directly on me and the other partners," retorts the partner. "After all, if the firm is to blame, then surely some of its personnel are as well. And since we partners are in control, and ultimately have the responsibility, in blaming the firm, as everyone knows, you are blaming us."

Now suppose that the spouse backs off, explaining that in blaming the firm, blame was not directed intentionally at any of the personnel in it.

"But if the firm is truly to blame, then somebody in it is to blame," continues the partner, "and everyone knows that includes me and the other partners."

The spouse, at this point, presses on, supporting a combination of ~1 and ~3. The spouse says:

"Look, I know full well that you are not to blame, and that none of the partners are either. I know that you were too busy to concern yourself with administrative details such as fire and disaster insurance policies. I recognize that the success of the firm required your full attention to your job. I admit that all the partners were in the same boat as you. I grant that what happened was, in the end, really no one's fault. It was all just a lot of bad luck."

How is such an exchange to be concluded? What might the partner reasonably say or think? Does it make sense for the spouse to proceed, given these admissions, to try to defend the blaming of the firm? That is, why blame the firm?

The answer here is that the spouse might continue to defend the propriety of blaming the firm while denying the relevance of the dependency thesis and denying that anyone is in any way to blame for the disaster. The spouse might act, at this point, out of pride and the wish to save face. This, however, is no vindication of the claim that the firm is to blame.

It is not difficult to imagine the course which such a dispute might follow from here.

"Well," responds the partner, "if you admit that no one was to blame, then you should not blame the firm."

"But that is exactly what deserves the blame," replies the spouse. "The blame falls on the firm, not on any of you, or anyone else."

Aware of the significance of the dependency thesis, the partner might well proceed from here to state the arguments formulated in sections 2.2 and 2.3. And assuming, perhaps improbably, that the argument remains on an honest intellectual level, how might the spouse reply? There are several possibilities. First, the spouse might admit the truth of dependency, and that since no individuals are to blame, neither is the firm. The spouse might thus recant, and acknowledge that the blaming of the firm was done in ignorance of the dependency thesis. This, of course, would be backing down and admitting that the blame was based on a misconception. The spouse would be acknowledging that the intended meaning of the blame is not supportable by the evidence, and is therefore untenable.

A second response of the spouse might be that although dependency is true, there is a different sense in which the firm is to blame. It should have been organized differently, although no one is to blame for not having done so. Such a view may reveal a subtle shift in the meaning of the spouse's blame. As the argument in 2.2 and 2.3 reveal, such blame must be lacking in typically moral content. That is, to claim that the firm should have been organized differently, but no one was to blame for the failure to try to alter the organization, is like claiming that a corporation was responsible for polluting at a time when all its personnel were gone. As explained in 2.1 and 2.2, such a statement is morally vacuous. Whether the spouse's blame was originally intended to be of a typically moral kind, it does not, under this interpretation, have significant moral content. Although the spouse might maintain that this is still a moral blame, it is inexplicable how it could be.

Similar examples could be constructed to reveal the incoherence of intending or believing, by a claim of organizational blame, any of ~1 through ~5. The point here is that either the claim is an inadequate formulation of one's actual intended meaning or belief, or the intended meaning is lacking in moral force. The five conditions mark the extremes of both significant moral purpose and intended meanings of attributions of organizational moral blame.

### 4.6 Purposes, Distribution, Evidence, and Meaning as Methodology

Questions concerning attributions of moral blame to an organization have been divided into several different categories: the purposes of such blame, the evidence needed to support claims achieving those purposes, the distribution of blame, and the intended meaning of such attributions of blame. Considered in relationship to one another, the results of these analyses suggest a strategy for appraising attributions of organizational blame.

To a statement that an organization is to blame for something, one may first investigate the evidence available. Assessment of that evidence allows one to determine whether or not the five conditions are fulfilled to a reasonable degree in the case at hand. If they are not, then the claim is spurious, and one needs to revise either its meaning, reference or one's purposes in making it.

If the five conditions are judged to be satisfied to a reasonable degree by the case at hand, one may judge initially that the moral claim is warranted. If one does so, one may either leave it at that, asserting the claim and inquiring no further, or one may pursue further efforts of clarification and evaluation. If one judges that the claim is warranted, one might want to clarify its meaning. To do this, one may inquire about the distribution of the claim. Whatever it may be, one is now faced with the need to make a further evaluation. One must now try to determine the extent to which the evidence supports the blameworthiness given the stated distribution.

What should one do if the five conditions are judged satisfied by the evidence at hand, yet there is no clear indication of the intended distribution? Suppose, that is, that the person attributing blame to the organization does not have any clear intentions about just who is to blame. If the evidence points to the likelihood of certain personnel or a certain group of them who are to blame, then they may be suggested as likely candidates for the intended distribution. But if the person making the statement is still unsure, then one must conclude for the time being that matters of distribution are unclear.

If the distribution is unclear, but the five conditions are judged fulfilled in the case at hand, then there is a likely candidate for questions of intended distribution. This is, as argued in 4.2, some indefinite group of individuals within the organizational network whose blameworthiness stems in part from their roles, purposes, and interconnections within the organization. To make this statement is not to grant, however, that there is any advantage to acknowledging the existence of one interpretation of distributivity over another. As the first four sections of this chapter reveal, distributivity is a question of intent. The five conditions can accommodate great variations in the intended distribution and meaning of these claims when made by different individuals with different purposes in different situations.

Examination of an example helps to clarify some of the points established in this chapter. Suppose that you have just finished watching a football game in which the Bears, one of the top-ranked teams in the league, have lost to the Packers, whose prior record has placed them firmly in the cellar. Although the Bears fans are generally disgusted at the poor play by the Bears, you, a Packer fan, are delighted by the Packers' win. A friend of yours, however, correcting your viewpoint that this was a great victory for the Packers, insists that the Bears are to blame for losing the game. Indeed, your friend goes on to indicate a profound disgust with the Bears' performance. As the discussion continues, it seems clear that your friend has a sort of moral indignation over the Bears' performance.

Suppose that you continue to disagree with your friend, and decide to pursue your case. You point out that not all the Bears played poorly, and that the Bears' fullback was the leading runner of the game. Your friend demurs, but still maintains that the Bears are to blame. In doing so, the friend is admitting that the evidence does not support a distributive interpretation of the attribution of blame.

You next address the question of whether the Bears as a whole, a unity, are to blame. You argue that the loss was surely not the coach's fault, and that there was nothing wrong with the Bears' game plan, or with player substitutions, or with the decisions of the referees. Again, your friend demurs, but still blames the Bears. In this demurral, your friend may be admitting that the fault of the Bears was not due to the malfunctioning of the team's internal decision structure. And this is tantamount to admitting that the evidence you have fails to show that the Bears, conceived in a Frenchian manner, is to blame.

You presume at this point that your friend must intend by the blame some nondistributive version of the claim. You then pursue further the question of just which Bears did and did not play well. It soon becomes clear that you and your friend agree that the wide receivers and the tight ends played poorly, but disagree about the quality of the play of the Bears' offensive and defensive lines. You and your friend still disagree about the overall assessment of the game. Your friend insists that this does show that the Bears are to blame for losing the game. You believe that the wide receivers, the tight ends and perhaps the linesmen played poorly. You then go on to point out all the fine play on the part of the Packers. You conclude that some of the Bears are partly to blame for losing the game, but that it is a mistake to conclude that "the Bears are to blame." The discussion ends as many such disputes do: in total deadlock, each side with some plausible arguments to support its case.

Consider why the position of your friend is neither incoherent nor unsupported by the evidence. Your friend may well intend that it is proper to assert that the Bears are to blame, not simply the wide receivers, tight ends, and the linesmen. For the poor play of these groups of players may not be due simply to their own inadequacies. There are important connections between the poor play of these groups of players and the many varied and subtle interconnections among team players that make this group into a team. After all, others on the team are also implicated. The coach could have replaced the lagging players; the other players could have put more pressure on them in the huddle, etc. Furthermore, it appeared that even those who played well on the team did not play as well as they often do. In the view of your friend, it is an oversimplification to blame only the lagging players: a full understanding of the nature of the loss shows that the fault for it is better expressed by a statement that names the team as blameworthy. In the view of your friend, a non-distributive attribution of organizational blame which refers to the fault of some identified players and, in addition, further unidentified personnel best captures the likely truth of the matter.

In blaming the Bears, your friend, and you as well, appear to be distinguishing between the blameworthiness of some of the members of the team and the team. Note, however, that this distinction can be maintained and clarified without assuming either distributive intent, a theory of team personhood, or a theory of vicarious negligence. Blaming the team may amount to nothing more than blame directed at some definite or indefinite group of personnel within the team structure whose blameworthiness arose within and due in part to that structure and the various subtle roles and interconnections which characterize football teams.

### 4.7 Chapter Summary

Questions of the distribution and meaning of attributions of organizational blame have been addressed occasionally and briefly in the first three chapters. This chapter develops a more focused approach to such questions in light of the foregoing analyses. The five conditions do not dictate any one interpretation of the distribution of attributions of organizational blame, but do have direct bearing on other questions of the meaning of such claims.

The first section argues that one who attributes blame to an organization may intend by this to be blaming all of its personnel. Such intended meaning does not contradict the sufficiency thesis, which states a requirement of evidence, not meaning. It is possible for one to have too much evidence for such intended meaning to be advantageous or advisable.

The second section shows how the five conditions permit organizational blame to be distributed to some but not all of the personnel in an organization. Thus, one may intend to refer to some specific individuals in the organization, to some indefinite group of individuals in it, or to be attributing vicarious negligence as suggested by Larry May. One may have coherent purposes to intend any of these. However, in the absence of a clear distributional intent, it appears that the five conditions themselves suggest the likelihood that the best candidate for an intended referent is some indefinite group of personnel within the organizational structure.

The five conditions also allow one to blame an organization without blaming any of its personnel. The third section recognizes a limited version of some of Peter French's work, which is further criticized in the next chapter. French can be credited with demonstrating that it may be reasonable to blame an organization without blaming any of its personnel. A limited version of a theory of corporate moral personhood may establish the plausibility of intending a claim of organizational blame to attribute blame to an entity referred to as "the organization."

The fourth section shows that the five conditions allow one to intend an attribution of organizational blame to be entirely nonreferential. Such intentions are, however, somewhat improbable. However, the important point is that the five conditions do allow the possibility that one may have purposes for making a statement which attributes blame to an organization, while actually intending the blame to have no real object or referent.

The implications of the five conditions for understanding the meaning of claims of organizational blame are spelled out in the fifth section. The argument of the first three chapters reveals that it would be indefensible to level moral blame at an organization and mean by this something which contradicted any of the five conditions. But such considerations provide no reason to think that all statements of organizational blame need to have the same meaning. Diversity of distribution and meaning go hand in hand, and are well accommodated by the five conditions.

A clear understanding of the five conditions and their import for questions of distribution, intended meaning and evidence reveals their value in assessing attributions of organizational blame. The sixth section shows briefly how the points of this chapter may help guide one through an attempt to understand and assess such attributions. The discussion in these first four chapters reveals that an analysis that provides strategies for clarifying and assessing diverse versions of such claims is likely to be more accurate, comprehensive, and enlightening than one directed to reveal some supposed single, true meaning.

**Notes**

1. Larry May, *The Morality of Groups* (Notre Dame, IN: University of Notre Dame Press, 1987), 83-89.

2. For others who largely accept such a limited version of French's work, cf. Kenneth E. Goodpaster, "Commentary," *Business and Professional Ethics Journal* 2, no. 4 (1983): 100-103; Virginia Held, "Corporations, Persons, and Responsibility," in *Shame, Responsibility and the Corporation,* ed. Curtler, 159-181; Kurt Baier, "Moral, Legal, and Social Responsibility," in *Shame, Responsibility and the Corporation,* 183-195; Patricia H. Werhane, "Corporate and Individual Moral Responsibility: A Reply to Jan Garrett," *Journal of Business Ethics* 8 (1989): 821-822.

# Chapter 5

## Being Before Blaming: Corporate Moral Personhood

The reasoning supporting the sufficiency and dependency theses is not based on any specific theory of the nature of organizations. This reasoning does not assume that organizations have any particular ontological structure, or differ in other than ordinary ways from other kinds of social groups. Rather, this approach treats attributions of organizational blame as whole linguistic expressions needing to be understood within the contexts in which they occur. Conditions of evidence for the plausible assertibility of such attributions have thus been clarified independently of questions of the nature of their referent.

Others approaching questions of group and organizational moral responsibility have started from the opposite direction, first addressing the nature of groups and organizations, and then questions of how they can be morally responsible. The work of Peter French is a clear and influential example of this approach. French's theory of corporate moral responsibility is based on a sharp distinction between two kinds of human collectivities. The grounds for drawing the distinction also provide grounds for understanding how corporations can be morally responsible. French argues that they can because they are in fact moral persons.

If French's theory were unobjectionable, one might consider the present analysis based on sufficiency and dependency to be superfluous. After all, French's analysis appears to provide clear and direct answers to questions of the meaning and justification of corporate and collective moral responsibility. However, the ontological basis of French's theory is the source of some serious inadequacies. These in turn reveal the shortcomings of basing a theory of

organizational blame on a set of ontological claims about collectivities of
various sorts.

French's theory is based on a distinction between two kinds of collectivities:
aggregates and conglomerates. The problem with his approach is illuminated
by two empirical inadequacies of this distinction. First, there are examples of
aggregates which possess the characteristics French claims are typical of moral
persons and unique to conglomerate collectivities. Second, the corporations
French claims are conglomerates show evidence of being aggregates. These
two inadequacies reveal that the distinction between aggregates and
conglomerates is best viewed as a distinction of degree, not kind.[1] Further and
more important, the inadequacies point to a fundamental flaw in French's
analysis of collective moral responsibility. They reveal that the distinction
between conglomerates and aggregates fails to differentiate actual human
collectivities. Consequently, the distinction is, in the end, of no help in
determining whether some collectivities are moral persons and some are not. It
lacks the capability for which it was developed.

## 5.1 Two Kinds of Collectivities: Aggregates and Conglomerates

French offers what one may refer to as the "membership criterion" to
distinguish aggregate from conglomerate collectivities. He defines an aggregate
as a collection of people such that a change in its membership is sufficient to
change its identity. "A change in an aggregate's membership will always entail
a change in the identity of the collection."[2] One's neighbors, teenage gangs,
and mobs are cited as examples of aggregates. Claims such as, "The mob
lynched the suspect," assert that the group comprised of a specific list of people
performed the lynching. The nature of that group is defined, French explains,
by the combined identities of its individual members.[3]

French defines a conglomerate collectivity, on the other hand, as "an
organization of individuals such that its identity is not exhausted by the
conjunction of the identities of the persons in the organization. The existence
of a conglomerate is compatible with a varying membership."[4] He cites clubs,
political parties, universities, corporations, and armies as examples of
conglomerates, and argues that "what is predicable of a conglomerate is not
necessarily predicable of all of those or of any of those individuals associated
with it. . . ."[5]

It is important to recognize that French offers the membership criterion as
the single mark that distinguishes aggregates from conglomerates. Referring to
it as an "identifying characteristic," he finds it wholly adequate to determine
whether particular collectivities are aggregates or conglomerates.[6] The
membership criterion does not alone, however, reveal that conglomerates are
moral persons while aggregates are not. French establishes the moral
distinction by adducing a further set of characteristics.

French claims that all conglomerates have "three significant characteristics" that "are not found in the case of aggregates." They have, first, internal organizations and decision procedures; second, enforced standards of conduct that are more stringent than standards that apply outside the conglomerate; and third, the presence of defined roles by virtue of which some members of the conglomerate "exercise certain powers over other members...."[7] These three will be referred to as the "three significant characteristics."

French goes on to argue that the three significant characteristics reveal that moral responsibility cannot be "legitimately ascribed" to an aggregate.[8] He holds that moral responsibility can only be legitimately ascribed to an individual person, and that an aggregate is not a person. Statements that appear to ascribe blame to an aggregate must be understood as a shorthand device summarizing the blame attributable to each member of the aggregate.[9]

French argues, on the other hand, that an attribution of moral responsibility to a conglomerate does not require the possibility of ascribing responsibility to any of the individuals associated through it.[10] This raises the question of how one could attribute moral responsibility to a human collectivity if none of the individuals associated through it is morally responsible for the matter at hand. If moral responsibility is attributed only to moral agents, and it need not be attributed to any in a conglomerate, then how could it be attributed to the conglomerate? French answers that one can attribute moral responsibility to conglomerates because they are in fact moral agents which he calls "persons."[11]

The three important characteristics of conglomerates reveal that they are, he argues, intentional systems, and their intentionality is logically independent of the intentions of the individuals associated through the conglomerate.[12] That is, the conglomerate may have an intent of its own that differs from that of any of its personnel. This intentionality is evidenced by the functioning of an internal decision structure. The structure, characterized by the three significant characteristics, is what French calls a "redescription license." It allows one to redescribe the functions of the conglomerate as its intentional actions. The internal decision structure is thus the metaphysical basis of the personhood of a conglomerate collectivity.

An internal decision structure is a complex of rules, procedures, roles and customs by which individuals associated through the conglomerate arrive at decisions that constitute the policies of the conglomerate. By exercising the powers of their offices according to the established procedures of a corporate conglomerate, the individuals in those offices contribute to the making of corporate decisions and the carrying out of corporate policy. The presence of an internal decision structure permits "both redescriptions of events as corporate and attributions of corporate intentionality. . ." and thus corporate moral responsibility.[13]

To argue merely that claims of moral responsibility have different meanings when attributed to conglomerates and aggregates would be a modest position. French, however, is not content with such fare. He concludes that conglomerates may be the subject of moral predicates attributable to persons, and that they are literally moral persons as much as humans, while aggregate collectivities are not.

The strategy of French's argument is important. First he argues that aggregates and conglomerates can be distinguished by the membership criterion. Next he argues that conglomerates have three important characteristics that are sufficient to establish that they are intentional systems in a typically personal sense. Since aggregates do not have the three characteristics, conglomerates are moral persons and aggregates are not. Thus, the distinction between aggregates and conglomerates turns out to be a moral distinction.

## 5.2 The Inadequacy of the Three Important Characteristics

The distinction between conglomerates and aggregates is empirically inadequate on two levels. First, the three significant characteristics fail to demonstrate that all aggregates have a different moral status from conglomerates. Aggregates that French presents as paradigm cases may well possess the three significant characteristics despite French's disclaimer. Second, the membership criterion does not successfully distinguish two types of collectivities. The examples French offers as paradigm cases of conglomerates show evidence of being aggregates.

The empirical inadequacy of the three significant characteristics is clearest if one assumes, temporarily, that the membership criterion successfully distinguishes aggregates from conglomerates. The problem is that the three significant characteristics often fail to reveal that aggregates are not moral persons. Aggregate collectivities may have the three significant characteristics which French holds are unique to conglomerates. Aggregate collectivities may thus have, on French's grounds, moral personhood.

The group of neighbors who watched passively as Kitty Genovese was assaulted and murdered is a case in point. French views the group as an aggregate, holding that its identity would change if any of its members were different.[14]   For that group to be an aggregate, according to the three significant characteristics, the group must lack either an internal decision structure, enforced standards of conduct, or defined roles by which power is wielded over others. That it is lacking in any such characteristics is not clear.

It is certainly true that none of the three are present in the group of Kitty Genovese's neighbors in a way as well defined as they are in a corporation. But this is not to grant that they are wholly absent. Sociological investigation might well reveal significant elements of the three characteristics in the group of neighbors.

The group may well have a rudimentary sort of decision procedure by which it functions. It might be, for example, that the lady on the second floor glanced up at the man on the third to note his reaction, and was cued to do nothing by his complacency. Had he made some sign, yelled to her, or yelled to the attacker, she might well have done something. It might be that every person who witnessed the murder would have gone running to Kitty's aid if the muscle man on the top floor had bellowed, "Let's get 'im!" The mere fact that there was no coordinated action that fateful day is no evidence that the neighbors totally lacked a decision-making network or structure. Nor is the fact that there is no such procedure in writing. Decision structures can develop spontaneously when people get together, for even very short times, and in the presence of weak relationships among them. Indeed, it this very kind of thing that sociologists and social psychologists report in their studies of group dynamics.[15]

In regard to the second of the three significant characteristics, there may well have been, among Kitty's neighbors, a relevant kind of enforced standard of conduct. The people in the apartment complex may all be familiar with the ideas of the talkative pacifist on the second floor, like and respect him, and avoid any behavior that would make them the brunt of his acid tongue. They may all seek to remain in the good graces of the apartment manager who has the absolute power to choose who among their friends are admitted to the apartment and which of them lose their leases. Enforcement of conduct takes place in varied and subtle ways, and there is no reason to think that all structure was totally absent in Kitty Genovese's neighbors.

Finally, it is quite likely that there was in the group the presence of defined roles by which certain powers are exercised over others. Perhaps there was a matronly lady on the fourth floor who bakes cookies for her neighbors, a man who is revered for his annual "open house" party, or a young woman who is a lawyer downtown, who once called a meeting of residents to discuss a problem with the landlord. Any such descriptions bespeak roles by which certain subtle kinds of power is wielded, and goals are achieved.

There are no realistic grounds to deny that the people in the apartment are united by common interests and directed toward common ends. They have much in common. In comparison to a corporation, they are certainly less structured. The point here is that they differ from a corporation mainly in degree of structure, common purpose and cohesion.

Similar points can be made even about mobs which assemble for limited periods of time. They are the objects of detailed sociological investigations which turn up varying degrees of structure. The three significant characteristics do not sort actual collectivities into discreet groups. They reveal, at best, differences of degree.

That some aggregates may have the three significant characteristics contradicts part but not all of French's analysis of collective moral responsibility. One might retreat from French's initial position by admitting that some aggregates may possess the three, but still argue that no conglomerates lack them. One might attenuate French's thesis and admit some aggregate collectivities to the ranks of moral persons. Even if the distinction between aggregates and moral persons is not as sharp as French indicates, there may be a clear and useful distinction among two types of human collectivities.

## 5.3 The Inadequacy of the Membership Criterion

There is, however, an empirical inadequacy of the distinction between aggregates and conglomerates that leads to further and more serious troubles for French's analysis of collective moral responsibility. This second inadequacy is independent of the question of moral personhood. It is an inadequacy of the membership criterion by which French distinguishes between aggregates and conglomerates.[16]    There is evidence that there may not be any distinct, unequivocal examples of either category. Beyond the view that the distinction between aggregates and conglomerates is one of degree, this is evidence that the two are not empirically distinguishable at all.

The empirical weakness of the membership criterion is apparent in French's treatment of business corporations. French argues that corporations are typical conglomerates for which changes in their personnel do not change their identities. He argues that company employees have confirmed this view by denying that their absence from the company would alter the company in any "essential" way. He points out that the component membership of Gulf Oil Corporation, for example, is so large that it is difficult to list, and that it is always in a state of flux.[17] He concludes that the identity of Gulf Oil is consistent with changes in its component membership, that its identity is not determined by its membership, and that it is a conglomerate as shown by application of the membership criterion.

Such reasoning ignores a counterargument showing that Gulf Oil may qualify as an aggregate by the membership criterion.    The fact that the corporation continues to be labeled "Gulf Oil" when some of its personnel change does not prove that a change in its personnel cannot change its identity. Our legal, social and linguistic convention of using the name "Gulf Oil" to label a corporation in 1996 and to label one in 1986 is, by itself, little proof that the two things have the same identity. For French to assert that the label "Gulf Oil" is a rigid designator that picks out the same object in every world[18] simply begs the question at issue. The question concerns the nature of the referent of "Gulf Oil." The question is whether any changes in its membership list are sufficient to justify the claim that the identity of the thing named "Gulf Oil" at one time is different from the identity of the thing named "Gulf Oil" at another time.

There is empirical evidence to show that a large enough change in membership alone can produce a change in the identity of a corporation such as

Gulf Oil. Consider the retirees of ten years ago who shake their heads and say "It just isn't the same company." Are they merely speaking elliptically? Suppose Gulf is convicted in court of some illegal (and morally repugnant) practice that originated after they retired, and that there have been no other major changes in company policies or procedures since their retirement. The retirees might still insist that it is now in important respects a different company because of extensive changes of personnel alone.

Any effort to refute the retirees' claim requires evidence that changes in personnel cannot change the identity of the corporation. The question arises as to what such evidence might be. One might, at this point, be tempted to adduce the three significant characteristics to help make the case. One might argue that even though all the personnel changed, the policies, procedures and corporate culture remained the same. In the present context, such reasoning cannot succeed.

Sameness of policies, procedures, and culture is not *ipso facto* sameness of corporate identity. The three significant characteristics cannot be used to demonstrate sameness of corporate identity unless they are adopted as the sole sufficient condition for the identity of a corporation. However, if one holds that they are, one has *replaced* the membership criterion as the necessary and sufficient condition of corporate identity and thus made a self-defeating move.

French offers the membership criterion as the single, necessary, and sufficient condition for determining whether a corporation is an aggregate or a conglomerate. To use the identity of policies, procedures, and corporate culture as sufficient to draw the distinction in a given case is to shift ground. It is to set aside the membership criterion and replace it with the three important characteristics as the determining factor in drawing the distinction.

The lesson at hand is that appeal to any properties (other than membership) to demonstrate sameness of identity is to grant that membership is not in fact a sufficient condition to distinguish actual aggregates from actual conglomerates. However, any challenge (such as that of the retirees) to the verdict of the membership criterion requires one to adduce further properties. That is, one must argue that other properties of the collectivity in question show that it is an aggregate or conglomerate. In doing so, one tacitly admits that membership does not suffice to establish identity. Therefore, admission of the mere plausibility of such challenges demonstrates the incapacity of the membership criterion to categorize actual collectivities.

The retirees' objection reveals that determinations of sameness of identity depend in part on social conventions. It is for purposes of investment, taxation, debt, inheritance, legal redress, reputation, public relations, etc., that Gulf Oil is considered the same corporation today as it was years ago. It is for these reasons, due not just to the inner metaphysical structure of a corporation, that the name, "Gulf Oil," is used as a rigid designator. French ignores the possibility that there may be strong reasons to question the value of such purposes, the identity of a given collectivity, and the ongoing use of its name as a rigid designator. Thus, whether or not Gulf Oil is a conglomerate by the membership criterion is not a categorical matter. Rather, it depends upon the priorities and purposes adopted in a given context.

The membership criterion is empirically inadequate in the sense that it does not in fact apply to collectivities on purely empirical grounds. To defend application of the criterion to specific collectivities requires consideration of one's purposes for holding that a change in membership does or does not change the identity of a collectivity. If a corporation is now charged with a serious crime for which the retirees feel innocent, they may claim that the extensive change in the corporation's personnel since they retired has been sufficient to change its identity. If, on the other hand, they are proud of the record it continues to build after they retire, they may argue that the corporation has changed membership but not identity. Moreover, one might argue that the identity of any human collectivity would change given a large enough change in its membership, and given an appropriate purpose to attribute such a change. Thus, the membership criterion, alone, is insufficient to distinguish any actual instances of conglomerate collectivities.

The empirical inadequacy of the membership criterion is no mere line-drawing problem. It is not merely an issue of a few unclear cases. It is a question of whether the examples French offers are genuine, and thus whether, in the end, there are any clear cases at all. If not, the criterion is conceptually as well as empirically inadequate.

One might, of course, point out that the membership criterion conceptually unproblematic because it is consistent and intelligible to imagine a distinction between aggregates and conglomerates as drawn on the basis of the criterion. But if every case adduced as an example is open to question on pragmatic grounds, the criterion is of doubtful value. If it draws a distinction without a clear referent, it is of no clarificatory value in the making of individual moral judgments about corporations.

The purpose of the membership criterion is to assist us to draw a line between human collectivities that are moral persons and those that are not. French holds that once we understand that all conglomerates have the three significant characteristics, we can merely identify a particular conglomerate, concluding that it is a moral person and that it is morally responsible for whatever it may have done. The objection here is that the membership criterion offers no clear basis to facilitate positive identification of any particular conglomerate. Whether a corporation is a conglomerate (as indicated by the membership criterion) is not discernible by examination of its empirical characteristics. Such categorization requires, in addition, a claim about the relevant purposes of those whose judgment is accepted as the basis for applying the membership criterion. It is the purposes of those who claim that change in its membership does or does not change its identity which is at issue. That various parties have different purposes and thus give different answers to the question is clear. The point is that the membership criterion alone draws no clear line, either in actual or hypothetical cases. It draws a distinction without a referent, and is therefore unhelpful in clarifying moral discourse.

## 5.4 A Pragmatic, not Empirical Distinction

One might defend French's analysis by maintaining that the present arguments prove only that the distinction between aggregates and conglomerates is a distinction of degree. Perhaps the distinction is not razor sharp. But it is never the less significant. Corporations are conglomerates and mobs are not. Corporations survive massive layoffs and retirements to maintain their corporate identities, while mobs that lose their members take on different identities. Although lacking empirical precision, the distinction between aggregates and conglomerates does not violate common sense, common language usage, or conceptual norms. It is a plausible theory that explains our inclination to say that a corporation is morally responsible even when none of its personnel are. This inclination is based on its characteristics as a conglomerate, not an aggregate.

Such a defense misconstrues the import of the above arguments. Whether a corporation is a conglomerate or an aggregate is determined not by its characteristics alone, but by additional consideration of human purposes. The verdict in specific cases depends on which purposes one adopts. Depending on what they are, use of the membership criterion could support the judgment that a given corporation is an aggregate. Moreover, an aggregate which is not a corporation might possess the three significant characteristics to a degree warranting the claim that it is a moral person and morally responsible. Either case reveals that whether a collectivity is a conglomerate or aggregate is irrelevant to the question of whether it can be properly claimed to be morally responsible.

One might respond that to be a conglomerate is morally significant because any such collectivity has the three significant characteristics and thus an internal decision structure. Such a claim could mean either of two things. First, it could mean that because the collectivity in question is a conglomerate, it has the three significant characteristics and thus an internal decision structure. Or second, it could mean that the collectivity in question in fact has them. However, neither construal successfully establishes that all conglomerate collectivities are moral persons.

Consider a corporation in a state of anarchy, with its decision procedures askew, its personnel confused and demoralized, and its organizational structure and policies wantonly violated by an indeterminate number of its personnel. Such a state of affairs might only last a short time. But while it lasts, there is good reason to continue describing this disorganized mess as a corporation.

And there might also be reason to describe it as a conglomerate (by application of the membership criterion). However, one might argue that it lacks the three significant characteristics and thus an internal decision structure. Such a corporation might be best described as a conglomerate without an internal decision structure and without a basis for a claim of moral personhood. It simply is not clear either that conglomerates must have the three significant characteristics and thus an internal decision structure or that they in fact do.

The very criteria French defends reveal that the status of a collectivity as a conglomerate is irrelevant to its status as a moral person. Moral personhood is determined, for French, by the presence of the three significant characteristics, while the membership criterion determines whether a collectivity is a conglomerate. These two sets of criteria are neither coextensive nor logically or conceptually connected.

A weakened version of French's position might claim that almost all conglomerates are moral persons and that most aggregates are not. Such a position does not, however, escape the problem of the membership criterion. That problem is not merely a problem of gray areas or borderline cases. The problem is one of indeterminacy. There are no empirical properties which can distinguish aggregates from conglomerates. They are distinguished only on the basis of the membership criterion, which depends on the purposes one adopts as decisive. If those purposes vary from corporation to corporation, so does the verdict of whether a particular collectivity is an aggregate or conglomerate.

The problem, then, is that the categories of aggregates and conglomerates lack a fixed extension. Their extensions are indeterminate. There is no way of knowing or deciding, from minute to minute, which collectivities are properly characterized as conglomerates and which as aggregates. If we adopt one set of purposes at one time as determining whether membership changes alter identity, these purposes may differ at the next, as the circumstances differ (depending, for example, on whether we are proud or disgruntled retirees).

Finally, it can, as a consequence, make no clear sense to assert that most conglomerates are moral persons. Lacking a clear method of sorting conglomerates from aggregates, we have no basis on which to assert anything about *most* conglomerates. We can, certainly, identify a collectivity and make a relatively plausible case for categorizing it as a conglomerate. We could argue at length, as French does, that it is unjustifiable at present to view a change in its membership as changing its identity. But our case would be based not simply on the application of criteria or certain characteristics of the collectivity, but on agreement regarding purposes relevant to deciding whether membership changes identity. There is no basis here for generalizations about conglomerates because conglomerates do not comprise a category determined by empirical properties.

## 5.5 The Argument's Fundamental Flaw

The strategy of French's argument is revealing. To identify a distinction between two kinds of collectivities and then argue that it is a moral distinction is in itself not promising. Consider as an analogy the distinction between cats and humans. That such a distinction can be drawn with biological criteria is clear. That such a distinction is a moral distinction is not. It is not clear that all and only humans are persons. There is a strong case to be made that neither brain-dead humans nor anencephalic humans are persons in the moral sense. And one theoretically could use genetic engineering to create critters that are biologically felines but are so intelligent that they are persons in the moral sense. In short, it seems unlikely that any distinction between two kinds of empirical objects will be coextensive with the distinction between persons and nonpersons.

Any attempt to demonstrate that the cat-human distinction is a moral distinction would require two sets of criteria. It requires one set to distinguish cats from humans, and another to distinguish persons from nonpersons. It also requires an argument demonstrating that the two sets of criteria are either coextensive, applying to all empirical cases in the same way, or that they are conceptually connected. That they are neither comes as no surprise. That the aggregate-conglomerate distinction and the person-nonperson distinction are neither conceptually connected nor coextensive is no less surprising.

There is, however, a difference between the cat-human distinction and the aggregate-conglomerate distinction that illuminates the problem with the latter. Although cats and humans can be empirically distinguished, aggregates and conglomerates cannot. They are distinguished on pragmatic grounds. To claim anything about conglomerates is, therefore, to make a claim based on pragmatic, not empirical considerations. It is to say that there is a category of collectivities called "conglomerates" such that all of them are moral persons, although we have no empirical properties for identifying any actual examples of such a category. The lack of empirical properties for the aggregate-conglomerate distinction is a major stumbling block. It is a reason to think that there is less hope of establishing aggregates and conglomerates as a moral distinction than cats and humans.

To assert that humans are persons is a statement whose accuracy can be determined by empirical investigation. One first uses empirical criteria to identify humans, and then determines whether they possess the criteria of personhood. However, it is impossible, as we have seen, to identify conglomerates on empirical grounds. Cases considered in all such attempts will be indeterminate in nature. If a number of clear cases could be found, one could then apply the three significant characteristics to determine which are moral persons. But in the absence of clear cases, there is no basis for any judgment at all about the makeup of actual conglomerates. Just what counts as a conglomerate and as an aggregate is empirically indeterminate. Therefore, the distinction can be of no help in determining whether some human collectivities are moral persons and some are not.

The argument here allows the possibility that corporations may be moral persons. The three characteristics might indeed serve as criteria of moral personhood in human collectivities. However, they do not divide such collectivities into two distinct groups. Such bifurcation was the promise of the membership criterion. Without it, the three significant characteristics can establish no more than degrees of collective moral personhood and thus degrees of potential moral responsibility.

There is, however, no proof either that all disorganized collectivities lack moral personhood and thus moral responsibility of the kind possessed by corporations, nor that all corporations are moral persons. This raises the troublesome question of how to determine which corporations have the three significant characteristics to a sufficient degree to warrant treatment as moral persons. It seems likely in the end that if such a line is to be drawn at all, it is best drawn on the basis of one's purposes in blaming or punishing, not on a supposed sharp ontological boundary between two categories of collectivities.


## 5.6 Beyond Collective Dualism

The problems with French's distinction extend well beyond it, leading to a certain parochialism in his general theory of the moral responsibility of collectivities. The thesis that organizations can be morally responsible because they are moral persons is unduly restrictive in its account of moral discourse. This thesis allows one to blame a collectivity in only two cases: either it is an organization with an internal decision structure, or it is some group of people without one. If the former obtains, then one may blame the organization because it is a moral person. But if one blames a collectivity without an internal decision structure, then one must be attributing blame to each of the individuals within it. Whatever else one may think one is saying is, for French, either unimportant or misguided.

Despite French's disclaimer, this is in fact a thesis about the meaning of moral language or discourse.[19] It asserts that two kinds of claims of the moral responsibility of collectivities are significant. By omitting an account of other possible meanings, the theory implies that we must mean one of these two things.

Such a position is as offensive as it is dogmatic and counterintuitive. It is counterintuitive because it seems that some assertions of organizational blame are neither based on the aggregate-conglomerate distinction nor assert what French holds they must. In blaming a collectivity, one may well intend to blame neither all of its personnel nor to say something that has anything whatever to do with the fact that the collectivity that has been named has an internal decision structure.    One might well deny that its having such a structure provides any basis for one's blame.  This may well be true of one blaming the residents of Kew Gardens for Kitty Genovese's murder.    One might intelligibly blame the state government of Alaska for the *Exxon Valdez* disaster while insisting both that only a few officials are to blame and that the state government decision-making structure did not in fact fail in any way.

French's dualism is dogmatic in allowing only two possible meanings to a claim of the moral responsibility of collectivities.  It ignores the great flexibility and diversity of moral language, and the presence of vagueness, uncertainty, and complex motives and meanings in many moral expressions.  It does not illuminate or even allow for the meaningfulness of many vague, unclarified and unsupported moral assertions and even convictions about collectivities of various kinds in various situations.

French's dogmatism is offensive because it tells speakers of the language who think they mean something different that they must be wrong.  It asserts that either they do not mean something other than what French allows, or that if they do, their views are hopelessly obscure, confused, or insignificant.  Such a theory offers metaphysical clarity only at the expense of moral and linguistic diversity.

French's dualistic theory and its shortcomings result from his ontological inquiry.   The ontological inquiry presupposes that in order to be meaningful, declarative sentences must attribute properties to distinct entities.  This inquiry is a search for these entities to which moral responsibility is attributed.  The inquiry thus assumes that ontology determines meaning, and that the meaning of these attributions will be illuminated by understanding the nature of that to which they refer.   As a result, French finds no reason to investigate the possibility that the declarative sentences making such attributions may at times be figurative, elliptical expressions.   His commitment to the dualistic ontological theory of collectivities directs him to address such sentences as attributing moral responsibility to entities defined by the theory.  It is this dualistic ontology that leads him to neglect the diversity and flexibility of language and thought in contexts of organizational blame and to discount the importance of the urge to blame when one is unsure exactly who is to blame, for exactly what and why.

The analysis developed in chapters one and two proceeds from the view that in order to understand attributions of organizational blame, we must first investigate the reasons or purposes motivating one's attribution of such blame and then the minimal evidence needed to support one's claim.  This study may then suggest a set of conditions under which such attributions are made, regardless of what it is to which they refer.  The clarification and defense of these conditions then helps one to avoid neglecting the richness of the contexts and the purposes of the attributions being studied.   From this point on, speculations about reference, meaning, and related ontological issues may proceed with less of a threat from a narrow, analytic dogmatism.

The analysis in chapters one and two of the contexts and purposes of organizational blame account for an important phenomenon which French largely neglects. This is the fact that people at times witness things going wrong, know that people are somehow to blame, suspect that the culprits are located within a certain set of people and also suspect that their connections to some organization are an important clue to the whole phenomenon. We may level blame in such circumstances due in part to our ideas about such matters and also due to our frustrations and the urge to express our feelings. And such attributions need not be declared irretrievably irrational. Although they are supported by limited evidence and include a significant element of speculation, no more can be said of many other important statements and beliefs. Furthermore, such attributions may, after all, serve important and worthy purposes, stimulating thought, debate and even inquiry.

The theory resulting from the analysis of the first four chapters is, in a sense, broader than French's theory, and tolerant of the central intuition that motivates his approach. This is the notion, borne out in the law, that organizations are at times treated like individual moral beings, and that they function in some ways which are analogous to human action. Such ideas are not inconsistent with the analysis developed here. After all, there is reason to think that some people do blame organizations as if they are persons. Furthermore, the presence of internal decision-making structures may help support the plausibility of such claims. The present analysis suggests that one may intend such meaning, and that it may be plausible.[20] However, the circumstances under which one makes such claims should not contradict the sufficiency and dependency theses and the five conditions enumerated in 2.5.

## 5.7 Chapter Summary

Peter French's theory of corporate moral personhood would appear to be a prime competitor of the analysis of the first four chapters. That theory is based on a distinction between two kinds of collectivities: aggregates and conglomerates. A conglomerate can be morally responsible and thus blameworthy because it has an internal decision structure, and is therefore a moral person. An aggregate is simply a group of people, and claims that one is responsible attribute moral responsibility to each of its members, not to any unified entity. Despite the simplicity of French's conclusions, its ontological basis is profoundly and importantly inadequate.

The nature of conglomerate collectivities is defined by three important characteristics that are lacking in aggregates. In fact, however, many, and perhaps all collectivities have these characteristics to varying degrees. If so, then some aggregates have degrees of moral personhood. In addition, it seems likely that some conglomerates have differing degrees of moral personhood.

The criterion offered to distinguish aggregates from conglomerates in fact draws no sharp line between actual collectivities. According to this, the membership criterion, any collectivity whose identity remains the same if its membership changes is a conglomerate, and any whose identity changes is an aggregate. This criterion, however, is not applicable on empirical grounds. A given collectivity will fall in one or the other category depending on the purposes one has for granting that a change in its membership changes its identity. Therefore, the membership criterion is insufficient to sort actual collectivities into two distinct groups with distinct moral status. The status they have depends upon one's purposes at the moment. If different people may legitimately have different purposes, then the same collectivity may be a conglomerate from the perspective of one person and an aggregate from the perspective of another.

These problems with the theory of corporate moral personhood reveal that no one collectivity can be known definitively to be a conglomerate or an aggregate. Indeed, examples reveal that a given collectivity may have elements of both categories to varying degrees. French's distinction thus provides no clear basis for a bifurcation of claims of the moral responsibility of collectivities.

The shortcomings of the theory of corporate moral personhood offer important lessons for the analysis of organizational blame. To base such an analysis on an ontological distinction between types of collectivities is likely to limit the resultant understanding of related linguistic expressions. The diversity and flexibility of language usage in a wide variety of contexts may well resist an interpretation of meaning based on supposed distinct ontological realities.

People may blame collectivities of various sorts for many different reasons, meaning many different things by the use of similar linguistic expressions. To understand why people blame organizations, the contexts in which they do so should be clarified along with their purposes and the evidence they use to support their views. Conditions for their doing so should be drawn from these three main considerations, not from a supposed ontological stronghold. Attention to these three considerations leads to the analysis in the first four chapters and accounts for the flexibility and diversity of the views of those who blame the organization.

## Notes

1. Others who have argued for such a view are David Copp, "What Collectives Are: Agency, Individualism and Legal Theory," *Dialogue* 23 (1984): 249-269; Robert Ware, review of *Collective and Corporate Responsibility*, by Peter A. French, *The Philosophical Review* 96 (1987): 119.

2. French, *Collective and Corporate Responsibility,* 5.

3. *Ibid.,* 5, 21-26.

4. *Ibid.,* 13.

5. *Ibid.,* 13.

6. *Ibid.,* 13, 26-27.

7. *Ibid.,* 13-14.

8. *Ibid.,* 10.

9. *Ibid.,* 10-13, 25-26.

10. *Ibid.,* 13.

11. *Ibid.,* 38-47; French, "Principles of Responsibility, Shame and the Corporation," 36.

12. French, *Collective and Corporate Responsibility,* 43-47.

13. *Ibid.,* 46.

14. *Ibid.,* 7-12.

15. cf. Stanley Bates, "The Responsibility of 'Random Collections'," *Ethics* 81 (1971): 345.

16. For a careful analysis of the membership criterion and related issues, cf. John R. Welch, "Corporate Agency and Reductions," *The Philosophical Quarterly* 39 (1989): 409-424.

17. French, *Collective and Corporate Responsibility,* 27, 28.

18. *Ibid.,* 29-30.

19. French, *Collective and Corporate Responsibility,* xiii.

20. This position is compatible with the conclusion arrived at by Michael J. Phillips, "Corporate Moral Personhood and Three Conceptions of the Corporation."

# Chapter 6

## Vicarious Negligence as a Moral Theory

An extensive analysis of collective responsibility is developed by Larry May in the first four chapters of his book, *The Morality of Groups*. Like French, May bases his analysis on a study of the metaphysics of human collectivities. But unlike French, he finds no sharp ontological distinctions between different kinds of collectivities, concluding instead that they differ largely by degree. He argues that the members of mobs can have important common interests, and group solidarity, and thus a kind of prereflective intent.[1] As a result, a mob, as well as an organization, can be described by intentional and moral predicates, although such ascriptions do not have the same literal meaning as a claim that a given individual human is morally responsible.

May proposes the theory of corporate vicarious negligence as a model for understanding corporate moral responsibility. According to this view, a corporation is vicariously negligent and thus morally blameworthy for the harmful acts of one of its members if, roughly, the harmful conduct resulted from a corporate grant of authority, and some members of the corporation could and should have taken effective preventive measures. As plain and uncontroversial as this model may appear, May's discussion of the main questions of organizational blame is profoundly disappointing. The  trouble with May's approach is that it fails to address and answer many basic questions about the moral blameworthiness of organizations. At several fundamental points, the discussion avoids certain central questions, and at others it denies various answers which might offer some clarity. Moreover, consideration of his model in light of such questions offers little help. In the end, the extent to which May's approach is appealing can be accommodated within the analysis developed here in the first three chapters.

### 6.1 Summary of May's Analysis

May begins his study with the question, "What kind of entity is a social group?"[2]   He opposes a version of methodological individualism, arguing instead that it is mistaken to think that social groups do not exist.[3]   He opposes a version of methodological holism, including French's position, arguing that it is also mistaken to think that social groups exist in their own right, as full moral agents.[4]   Characterizing this latter approach as "radical collectivism," he argues that there is no good reason for positing the existence of social groups as superentities.[5]   Rather, he aspires to a middle position according to which "social groups are conceived as individuals *in* relationships."[6]   He argues that it is the mark of a social group that it enables its members to perform actions they could not have performed on their own.[7]   He concludes that "when a collection of persons displays either the capacity for joint action or common interest, then that collection of persons should be regarded as a group."[8]

It is important, May thinks, that groups of various kinds as disparate as mobs and organizations can be said to act.   But this group action is not the action of some super individual.   Rather, it is the combined actions of a number of human persons.

For actions by individuals to be described as group actions, they must be not simply a collection of actions of some list of individuals.   They must be in some way unified.   May argues that the presence of a solidarity relationship among group members can make it possible to treat the actions of individuals as if they were the actions of a single entity.[9]   Solidarity is the sense among group members of a common interest and purpose.   The actual development of solidarity among such members enables them to act in ways they previously could not.   When that solidarity is present among a collection of persons, the collection should be treated as a group, and actions resulting from the solidarity may be described as group actions, although they are in fact the actions of individuals influenced by the presence of a solidarity relation among them.

Solidarity can also serve as a basis for attributing intentions to groups.   May cites some of Sartre's work on prereflective consciousness and that of contemporary psychologists on unconscious intent to formulate the notion of prereflective intent.[10]   He maintains that individuals in groups can have pre-reflective intentions that are caused by their solidarity with the group.   Yet, although group members may not be aware of them, these prereflective intentions can motivate intentional action.

Although actions and intent can both be attributed to groups, May does not accept French's position that such attributions can be made literally.   Rather, he holds that "to say that there are collective intentions proper, that is, to say that the group can intend in just the same way that individual persons can intend, is a fiction."[11]    We say that groups act and intend because there are some similarities to the ways in which individuals act and intend.    But such similarities should not hide the fact that there are also important differences.

Since intent and action can be attributed to groups, May holds that moral responsibility can, as well.    But although he holds that it can make sense to attribute moral responsibility to groups, one must do so in a different way from that of attributing it to individuals.    May states repeatedly that in order to attribute moral responsibility to groups, one need not attribute personhood to them.[12]

May denies that ascriptions of moral responsibility to mobs are either what he calls "distributional" or "nondistributional."    That is, he denies that such ascriptions attribute responsibility either to all the members of a mob or to none of them.[13]    However, he does not in fact argue that such claims attribute it merely to some members of the mob.    Rather, he stops short of describing that to which such claims do attribute moral responsibility.    Indeed, he abandons the question of the intended reference of such claims.    He argues, instead, that in discussions of mobs, the important question is how responsibility should be assigned.    And here, he maintains that "since the intention is not a reflective state for most members, the members of mobs should not be held individually responsible for the harms caused by them."[14]    In the effort to distribute responsibility for harmful effects of mob actions, one should seek out mob leaders and those who played ". . . a key role in causally constituting the mob" and inciting it to act.[15]

May's treatment of corporate action, intent, and responsibility is directed to show that intentional and moral predicates can be attributed to organizations independently of whether they are special kinds of metaphysical or moral entities, such as persons.    His approach is based on the notion of vicarious agency.    This refers to the fact that the actions of the employees of a corporation can be said to be the acts of the corporation.    "The defining characteristic of the corporation, which allows one to say that it acts when others act for it, is set by the rules and procedures adopted and formally agreed to by the stockholders."[16]    The rules and procedures of the organization, then, determine which acts of its employees are to count, vicariously, as acts of the corporation.    Vicarious agency explains how a corporation can be said to act quite independently of the question of whether or not it is in some sense an intentional agent or a moral person.

If vicarious agency explains how a corporation can act and intend, what explains how the act of an individual can count as the act of the corporation or professional association?    This question is answered with the theory of apparent authority.    May explains apparent authority, a legal concept, as that condition that allows a given person to be understood by others to be acting as a representative of a group.[17]    It is authority based on the expectations of others and it assigns agency without requiring that the principal actually delegate any function to an individual.  "Apparent authority assigns agency without having to prove a causal connection between principal and agent . . . ."[18]  Thus, by virtue of apparent authority, one or more individuals can perform actions that are viewed as the actions of an organization and for which it is held to be responsible.

May argues, in addition, that intentional behavior can be attributed to a corporation without the need to establish that it is an intentional or moral entity in its own right.   Here, May agrees with French that corporate policies, procedures, and decisions do allow one to describe corporations as having intent.   He maintains, however, that there is no need to claim that they do so because corporations are intentional beings or moral persons.   Rather, May holds that the policies, procedures, and decisions of corporate employees show that there is a similarity between the intentional behavior of individual humans and the functioning of corporations.  This similarity and the relevant differences can be understood, however, in light of the theory of vicarious agency and with no need to lose sight of the fact that the putative corporate actions and intent are actually just some combination of those of individual humans.[19]  There is a basis for attributing action and intent to corporations, but that basis is individual humans, their relationships, actions, intentions, and neglect.

On the question of the moral responsibility of corporations, May takes a different approach.  He does not address questions of what is meant by making such attributions.   Nor does he analyze the many different situations under which people attribute corporate moral responsibility or the many different ways in which they do so.  Nor does he address the question of what conditions are necessary or sufficient for such a claim to be established.  Nor does he, finally, explore the kinds of evidence which might likely support such claims.

Rather, he asks what model for assigning corporate responsibility best addresses the shortcomings of treating the corporation as if it were a person on the one hand, and those of treating the corporation as if it were strictly liable on the other.[20]  The answer he gives is the theory of corporate vicarious negligence.  A vicarious action is an action performed by one person but attributable to someone or something else.

Having explicated the nature of corporate vicarious action, it requires little for May to clarify that of corporate vicarious negligence.  A corporation is, accordingly, vicariously negligent for the harmful acts of one of its members if (a) this person was enabled or facilitated in his or her harmful conduct by a grant of authority resulting from a corporate decision of some sort; and (b) appropriate corporate members failed to take appropriate preventive measures, and could and should have done so.[21]

May goes on to point out that this theory suggests a direction for establishing the moral responsibility of a corporation.   "For an act to be ascribed to the corporation there must be a decision made by high-ranking managers within the corporation and there must be an action taken by at least one of the employees of the corporation pursuant to that decision."[22]   Once these conditions and the conditions of vicarious negligence are fulfilled, one can attribute an act to a corporation and also moral responsibility for that act. However, in doing so, one is in fact attributing nothing more than vicarious negligence.

## 6.2 Vicarious Negligence and Reference

The problems with May's account are more problems of inadequacy than of error.  The indirectness and vagueness of his discussions lead him to avoid many questions of crucial and telling importance.  Specifically, he refrains from addressing directly questions of the purpose, meaning, reference, truth conditions, and evidential basis of claims of the moral responsibility of groups of various kinds.  As a result, one must speculate what his answers to such questions might be.  As this and the following sections demonstrate, some of these answers are likely to be unsatisfactory and others unhelpful.  In the end, his work offers no basis for a general theory of corporate moral responsibility.

Consider the nature of the referent of attributions of what May calls "collective moral responsibility."  Before proceeding, however, it is important to note that May identifies no fundamental difference between such attributions and those of what he calls "corporate responsibility."  Indeed, he says of his analysis that "the model I am proposing is that the corporation is treated not as a single entity but as a collection of entities . . . ."[23]  He asserts that his ". . . model of collective responsibility . . . is better able to deal with the most common cases involving harms attributed to corporations."[24]    That is, corporate responsibility is a special case of collective responsibility.  So, May's statements about the reference of collective responsibility may be taken to apply, as appropriate, to corporate responsibility as well.

May denies that claims of collective moral responsibility are either distributional or nondistributional.  In doing so, he is denying that such claims refer either to all or none of the individual humans in the collective.   In addition, of course, he opposes French's theory of corporate moral personhood, thus denying that such claims refer to the collective as if it were an individual person.  When moral responsibility is attributed to corporations, to what, then, is it being attributed?

Such an attribution could be referring to some of the individuals in the collective.  Perhaps it refers to those whose negligence is, vicariously, described as the fault of the collective.  However, in addition to the fact that May does not state that this is the referent of the attribution, it is difficult to understand how it could be.

Assume the following proposition for the sake of investigation: When one attributes moral responsibility to a corporation, one is attributing it to those related individuals whose negligence, vicariously, allows us to describe the collective as responsible for the harm in question. Now this is, on one level, plausible. One might, after all, intend to attribute moral responsibility to a few individuals in the corporation and simply be speaking elliptically (or carelessly) in actually saying that the corporation is responsible.

The problem lies in the fact that there are many cases in which it seems that people attribute responsibility to organizations but would deny that they intend to attribute it to individuals. And if so, then the proposition sheds no light whatsoever on these attributions. They are either unexplained by the proposition, or simply spurious. Thus, the theory of vicarious negligence does not provide a plausible referent for many claims of what May calls "corporate moral responsibility." It does not offer a basis for a general theory of the reference of such claims.

Suppose, then, that May were inclined to hold that claims of corporate moral responsibility in fact do not refer to anything at all. Perhaps they are purely elliptical expressions, explicable by the theory of corporate vicarious negligence. May does indicate that in attributing corporate moral responsibility, one is doing something different from attributing individual moral responsibility. He holds that corporations cannot be morally responsible in the same way that individuals can. Rather, he argues, corporations can only be said to be vicariously negligent. But since attributing collective moral responsibility does not refer to anything, the collective is not morally responsible for anything, although it may be vicariously negligent. So in attributing moral responsibility to a corporation, one is not in fact attributing moral responsibility to anything. One is simply attributing vicarious negligence to the corporation.

There are two serious inadequacies of such an approach. The first concerns the referent of claims of vicarious negligence. If one can attribute vicarious negligence to a corporation, it would appear that one is attributing it to something. Then what is it? May states that his theory of vicarious negligence treats ". . . the corporation not as a single entity but as a collection of entities or persons, some of whom grant authority to others, some of whom might harm others, and some of whom might act to minimize potential harm."[25] So vicarious negligence is attributed to a collection of persons in the corporation. Which persons? Does this collection include the secretaries or janitors? It would, of course, depend on the nature of the harm in question. If this was a harm to which they had no possible connection, it would, presumably, not. Therefore, vicarious negligence is attributed to some group of individuals in the corporation, but not to the corporation itself.

Such a position offers no answer to the question of why one bothers to attribute vicarious negligence to the corporation instead of the group of negligent individuals in the corporation. Neither does it explain why one might insist that the corporation, not just a group of individuals within it is vicariously negligent. By treating the corporation as a collection of persons and ignoring the significance of the very language of corporate vicarious negligence, the theory of vicarious negligence renders such language and thought inexplicable.

The second inadequacy of denying that there is a referent of claims of collective moral responsibility is that such denial fails to account for the language of organizational moral blame. At times, some people clearly intend to blame an organization but do not intend to be attributing vicarious negligence to some group of persons in it. Often, people blame an organization and yet admit that they have no idea of just who in the organization also deserves blame. They may admit that many of the prime suspects in it have real exculpatory excuses and are not in fact vicariously negligent. But if claims of collective moral responsibility have no referent and refer neither to individuals nor to an entity named "the organization," then it is a mystery as to what they could mean. To respond that they mean that it is vicariously negligent simply moves the same question one step back. Just what is vicariously negligent? A number of persons or some superentitity? Since May denies the latter possibility, he is stuck with a version of the former, together with its explanatory impotence.

The problems raised here are based on the view that it is a legitimate question to ask for clarification of the referent of claims of organizational moral blame. Perhaps it is not. But if so, then there is need for an explanation as to why such claims are not in fact referring expressions and how they can be meaningful even though they are not. The theory of corporate vicarious negligence offers no such explanations. It replaces one apparent referring expression with another and then closes off questions of why people in fact bother to use either one. Such an approach raises a many questions as it answers.

## 6.3 Vicarious Negligence and Conditions of Warranted Assertibility

One of the questions that May does not directly address is that of what conditions of evidence must be met in order to enable one to assert plausibly that a corporation or organization is morally responsible or to blame. Indeed, the model of corporate vicarious negligence is as close as he comes to suggesting such conditions. But this model falls short of providing them, and offers very limited assistance in the effort to determine whether or not a given corporation may be plausibly blamed.

The model provides two conditions under which a corporation is vicariously negligent for the harmful acts of one of its members. The conditions are, briefly, that (a) the member was enabled in the harmful conduct by a grant of corporate authority, and (b) some appropriate members of the corporation failed to take preventive measures and could and should have.[26] May writes as if these can be used as conditions for corporate moral responsibility.[27]

One shortcoming of this theory as offering truth conditions for corporate moral responsibility lies in its initial assumption that one already knows of the harmful acts of some corporate member. What if one lacks such knowledge or evidence? The theory of corporate vicarious negligence offers no means of addressing cases in which one lacks reliable knowledge of any such individual, yet has evidence that seems to support the view that the corporation is responsible. Cases discussed here in prior chapters regarding the pollution of the Prince William Sound, Hooker Chemical Company, and the spouses of the computer company partners have no place in this theory. In fact, May himself simply avoids any discussion of the issues in such cases, as if they are of no significance. The theory of corporate vicarious negligence thus offers no basis for adducing conditions of warranted assertibility for attributions of organizational moral blame.

### 6.4 The Meaning of Corporate Responsibility Claims

The limitations of May's discussion extend beyond his failure to clarify questions of reference and truth conditions. His work offers no coherent clarification of questions of the meaning of claims about corporate moral responsibility. The theory of corporate vicarious negligence offers an explanation of meaning only by fiat.

To the question of what it means to attribute moral responsibility to a corporation, May offers the theory of corporate vicarious negligence. That is, such attributions apparently mean, roughly, that some member of the corporation engaged in harmful conduct as a result of a grant of corporate authority, and that other members of the corporation could and should have tried to prevent it. Now the question at hand is how this answer explains the meaning of the claim that the corporation is to blame. The theory of vicarious negligence cites conditions under which a corporation may be vicariously negligent. But what is the connection between vicarious negligence and our ordinary expressions of corporate blame? How does it clarify their meaning?

Although one can answer this question on May's behalf in a number of possible ways, none is satisfactory. Consider first the response that the only coherent thing a claim of corporate blame could mean is that the corporation is vicariously negligent. As argued in prior sections of this chapter, such a view contradicts many instances and cases in which thoughtful people attribute corporate blame without the evidence that May thinks would establish vicarious responsibility. The diversity of our use of language, our thought, and our responses to endlessly varying situations contradicts the plausibility of such a strong construal of May's work.

If claims of corporate blame can, in some cases, have meanings other than vicarious negligence, one might respond, at least vicarious negligence is itself clear and coherent. That is, if people understand their claims of corporate blame as claims of vicarious negligence, they will have a clear understanding of what they are saying. It will be clear, moreover, what would be needed to establish the truth of their claims.

May's analysis does offer some clarity by specifying criteria for establishing a claim of corporate vicarious responsibility. The problem is that May fails to clarify a link between this and actual attributions corporate moral blame. He fails to show that the meaning of such attributions is captured by the theory of corporate vicarious responsibility. Indeed, he does not seriously investigate questions of the meaning of claims of corporate moral blame, and does not base his theory of vicarious negligence on any such analysis.

In the absence of such analysis, May's stance on the model of vicarious negligence suggests that we actually replace our thinking about corporate moral blame by our thinking about corporate vicarious responsibility. Suppose that the conditions of corporate vicarious negligence hold in a given situation. May's work offers no clear reason why one should say that the corporation is to blame, instead of simply that it is vicariously negligent. May himself seems to think, after all, that the latter is the clearer mode of expression.

Neither does May's discussion explain why one should blame the corporation instead of the individuals cited in the criteria of vicarious negligence. Neither reference to corporate authority nor to corporate roles implicates the corporation instead of individuals. The presence of corporate authority in such a situation involves little more than the fact that some individuals in the corporation granted this authority, and some failed in their duties. Corporate roles are simply the kinds of roles in which the corporate individuals acted. If these individualistic concepts indeed capture the realities of the situation, then why blame the organization?

Why not simply say that corporate employees, variously enmeshed in their corporate roles, are to blame? May fails to give any reason whatever to say anything else. He states at one point that ". . . we need to make reference to the group in order to explain the purposiveness of behavior displayed in certain cases . . . one cannot reduce talk of corporate policies and goals to talk of the individual members of the corporation."[28] But all he means by this, he states repeatedly, is that "social groups should be analyzed in terms of individuals in relationships."[29] And this, together with the theory of corporate vicarious negligence, indicates that, in May's view, corporate responsibility can be understood as a combination of the responsibilities of individuals which result from their corporate interrelationships.

Contrasting the approach of Peter French sharpens the shortcoming of May's answer to questions of meaning. French offers a clear and simple answer to the questions of what it means to blame a corporation and why one might do so. His position is that in blaming a corporation, one is blaming a being named by the term "corporation." The reason one can do this is because corporations can have intentions and be said to act. One can describe a corporation as a metaphysical person on grounds that are coherent and consistent with our thought about moral responsibility and metaphysical personhood. One is motivated to attribute such responsibility by the fact that there are acts which may be described as acts of the corporation, although no individuals are clearly responsible for them. So, French argues, what it means to blame the corporation is just exactly what it says: the corporation is to blame. One can attribute such blame for the very same kinds of reasons that one adduces to show that an individual human is to blame for something.

The theory of corporate vicarious negligence implies that what it means to blame a corporation is something other than what one appears to say. In doing so, one is not blaming a moral being, the corporation, but is attributing vicarious negligence. The problem is that if this is so, there is simply no good reason why one bothers to blame a corporation instead of its personnel. Those who do so must simply be speaking carelessly.

The analysis of the first three chapters of this book provides a clear and coherent basis for a number of answers to the question of what it means to attribute moral responsibility to an organization. Such answers may be offered depending on one's purposes. They need not exclude from the realm of possibility the answers given by both French and May. Thus, one may mean that one intends to blame the organization because one is thinking of it as a moral person; or one may be speaking elliptically and actually intending to attribute vicarious negligence; or one may mean that some indefinite group of individuals connected through the organization is to blame. And there are other possible interpretations.

In proposing his theory of corporate vicarious negligence as the best way "to treat" corporate moral blame, May obfuscates what exactly the theory is supposed to accomplish. He fails to understand the significance of the distinction between questions of meaning, questions of reference, and questions of truth conditions. As a result, his proposed theory of corporate vicarious negligence can amount to little more than a proposal that one could, if one chose, mean, in blaming a corporation, simply that the corporation was vicariously negligent. But he offers no significant reason to think that people always do mean this, or that they should. Nor does he demonstrate that such intended meaning would capture an important part of the meaning of ordinary attributions of corporate blame.

## 6.5 May's Work as a Special Case of the Five Conditions

Despite the many inadequacies of May's work, the present discussion should not be taken to reject it entirely. Vicarious negligence is, after all, one plausible way of viewing certain cases of corporate responsibility. What the present analysis has endeavored to show is that this theory cannot provide a comprehensive analysis of corporate moral responsibility or blameworthiness. It does not address and cannot answer all of the questions that are addressed in the analysis developed here in the first four chapters.

However, May's work can be viewed as a special case, a partial, sketchy version of the analysis developed in the first three chapters and summarized in 2.5. Although May does not directly address all the questions at the heart of that analysis, his work does assume answers to some, allow varying answers to others, and also provide answers to a few. In these, May's approach does not contradict the main tenets of that analysis.

May's analysis is developed to answer what he views as the central question regarding corporate responsibility. Toward the end of his initial discussion of vicarious agency, May states: "The biggest problem for a theory of corporate responsibility or liability is to ascertain when an employee, supervisor, or manager, etc., is acting on his or her own and when he or she is acting for the corporation."[30] The relationship of May's work to the present analysis should be understood in light of this question.

May's formulation of this question assumes that the actions of individuals can incur corporate responsibility. That is, it assumes right from the start that a corporation can be responsible due to the actions of its personnel. The central task for May, then, is to distinguish one's actions for oneself, which apparently do not incur the responsibility of the corporation, from one's actions for the corporation, which apparently do. The theory of vicarious negligence draws this distinction.

May's formulation of the important question is what leads him to avoid direct confrontation with the questions of the sufficiency and dependency theses. By assuming that the important issue is how individuals can be said to be acting for the corporation and thus incurring corporate responsibility, he co-opts these questions. That is, the question itself assumes that questions of corporate responsibility are questions of how individuals can make a corporation responsible. The fact that they do is not in doubt. Nor is the question of whether or not any individuals must be responsible in order for a corporation to be said to be responsible. May simply assumes that some individuals are responsible. The only remaining question for him is that of how the individuals warrant claims that the corporation is responsible.

By formulating the question as he does, and responding with the theory of corporate vicarious negligence, May appears to take a stand on the dependency thesis. He appears to hold that the only questions of corporate responsibility worth considering are those that arise when some individuals in the corporation have some contributory responsibility for the matter at hand. This approach appears to assume the truth of the dependency thesis. By doing so, there is, for May, no reason to examine the issues surrounding it, and no reason to argue for it. His work is not only consistent with it, but actually assumes its truth.

The important question, as May raises it, does not, however, clearly imply a stand on the sufficiency thesis. That question allows the possibility that all corporate personnel are to some extent responsible and that we know how they are. The question simply directs us to address the matter of how they make the corporation responsible. In regard to the sufficiency thesis, then, May's work offers no grounds contradicting the five conditions or the analysis supporting them.

May's formulation of the important question to be addressed regarding corporate responsibility leads him to take very seriously the issue discussed in section 3.2. That is the question of how and why it appears that certain actions performed in one's organizational role may reveal that the organization is to blame, while those performed on one's own do not. The argument in that section reveals that this and other related questions can be settled independently of the five conditions. May's answers to these questions are no exception to this position. Regardless of whether the theory of corporate vicarious negligence provides a satisfactory answer to that question, it does not contradict the analysis developed through the five conditions. Nothing in those conditions or the arguments establishing them prohibits the possibility of formulating concepts of group solidarity, prereflective intention, vicarious action, vicarious intention, or corporate vicarious responsibility. The five conditions can accommodate the theory of corporate vicarious negligence as a special further development of the philosophy of corporate moral responsibility. This chapter has sought to demonstrate merely that May's work does not offer the basis for a general theory of corporate moral blame.

## 6.6 Chapter Summary

The chapter is directed to demonstrate that the work of Larry May does not provide the groundwork for a general theory of corporate moral blame but that much of it can be retained as a special case of the conditions specified in 2.5 and supported by the analysis of the first three chapters.

The survey of May's argument in the first section of this chapter reveals that, like French, he begins his analysis from a study of the nature of collectivities and the role of individuals in them. He argues that a group of people may be said to act when there is a relationship of solidarity among them. Such a relationship also reveals the presence of prereflective consciousness and intentions which can motivate them, and which are caused by their membership in the group. As a result, we can attribute intentional action and thus moral responsibility to a group, although doing so is doing something different from attributing it to an individual human person.

May argues that intentional and moral predicates can be attributed to organizations for similar reasons. But unique to them are phenomena of vicarious agency. According to vicarious agency and the theory of apparent authority, corporate rules and procedures enable individual acts to be taken as the acts of the corporation. The presence of decision structures in a corporation allow one to attribute intentional behavior to it. But such attributions do not require that the corporation be viewed as a metaphysical person. And one may attribute moral responsibility to a corporation if one means in doing so that the corporation is vicariously responsible for the acts of its personnel.

The next three sections argue that May's analysis cannot offer grounds for a general analysis of the moral blameworthiness of organizations. Section 6.2 argues that his work closes out all coherent answers to the question of the referent of claims of organizational moral blame. By denying that such blame is distributional, nondistributional, or refers to a unitary thing, it is obscure as to what it could refer. Eliminating any intelligible referent prevents his theory of corporate vicarious negligence from allowing any explanation of what the intended referent of many ordinary claims of corporate blame could be.

The third section argues, briefly, that the theory of corporate vicarious negligence offers no help in efforts to formulate truth conditions for claims of corporate moral blame. By assuming that we already know some individuals in the corporation who are partially blameworthy, the theory simply dismisses cases discussed in the first four chapters of this book. May's approach appears to assume that there is no question of how a corporation could be blameworthy if one has no knowledge of specific blameworthy personnel.

The fourth section argues that the theory of corporate vicarious negligence offers no significant clarification of the meaning of claims of corporate moral blame. There is no clear reason to think that the meaning of many such claims in varying contexts is captured by that theory. Rather than clarifying such claims, corporate vicarious negligence would seem, rather, to replace them.

It is argued in the fifth section that the shortcomings of May's analysis are not sufficient reasons to reject it entirely. Indeed, the theory of corporate vicarious negligence proposes a plausible answer to the question of when the performance of personnel may reveal organizational blameworthiness. If understood properly, that theory and the bulk of May's work is consistent with and can be viewed as a special case of the analysis developed in the first four chapters and summarized by the five conditions.

**Notes**

1. Larry May, *The Morality of Groups,* 67.

2. *Ibid.,* 9.

3. *Ibid.,* 11-17.

4. *Ibid.,* 18-24.

5. *Ibid.,* 24-25.

6. *Ibid.,* 5.

7. *Ibid.,* 26.

8. *Ibid.,* 28-29.

9. *Ibid.,* 37.

10. *Ibid.,* 60-62.

11. *Ibid.,* 65, 67.

12. *Ibid.,* 70.

13. *Ibid.,* 76, 82-83.

14. *Ibid.,* 83.

15. *Ibid.,* 108.

16. *Ibid.,* 46.

17. *Ibid.,* 48.

18. *Ibid.,* 52.

19. *Ibid.,* 69-71.

20. *Ibid.,* 84.

21. *Ibid.,* 85.

22. *Ibid.,* 96.

23. *Ibid.,* 85.

24. *Ibid.,* 83-84.

25. *Ibid.,* 85.

26. *Ibid.,* 85.

27. *Ibid.,* 96.

28. *Ibid.*, 71-72.

29. *Ibid.*, 9.

30. *Ibid.*, 47.

# Chapter 7

## Blaming Organizations and Blaming Groups

The analyses of the first six chapters have focused largely on questions of blame directed at organizations. They have assumed that such questions can be answered apart from any sharp ontological distinction between organizations and other kinds of collectivities. This is not to deny, however that there are differences between these, or that blame directed at organizations may differ in meaning, reference, truth conditions and evidence from that directed at other collectivities.

A full understanding of the nature of organizational blame requires clarification of its relationship to blame directed at other collectivities. The present chapter explores two different approaches to this relationship. Part I addresses questions of the meaning, reference and evidence for such blame. That is, given an attribution of blame directed at some less organized collectivity, how should its meaning and reference be understood, and how should it be assessed in light of the available evidence? Part II addresses the questions of when blame is more appropriately directed to individuals, organizations or other collectivities. Given the presence of some untoward event, what considerations reveal that it is most reasonable to blame individuals, organizations or some other kind of collectivity?

### Part I The Meaning and Reference of Collective Responsibility

Many writers on the subject have maintained that attributions of blame directed at structured organizations are nondistributive and thus do not attribute blame to all individuals in the organization. They have maintained, in addition, that attributions of blame directed at other less organized collectivities are distributive, attributing blame to all the constituent individuals.[1] However, it was argued in chapter four that it is possible that organizational blame may sometimes be distributive in its intended meaning. Such a position does not, of course, deny that such blame is usually best construed as nondistributive. Indeed, the five conditions accommodate the possibility of both construals.

Part I of this chapter reaffirms that blame directed at less organized collectivities may well be construed as distributive. However, there are also cases in which one may plausibly intend such blame to be nondistributive. In both kinds of cases, the degree of group solidarity present may be, but is not necessarily, of significance.

## 7.1 Blaming the Mob

Many writers have held that blame directed at mobs is in fact blame directed at each of their component individuals. Examination of some cases of such blame may help to clarify the reasoning behind such a view. Mob violence by supporters of British professional football teams offers several perspectives that help illuminate the issues and answers.

One of the most interesting and thoughtful recent accounts of mob violence is developed by Bill Buford in his popular but serious account, *Among the Thugs*.[2] Buford describes, firsthand, numerous occasions, during the 1980s, in which he was present and participated in mob violence before, during, and after British professional soccer matches. He describes a profound fascination and attraction on the part of mob members to the power felt during times of mob membership, and to the all-encompassing thrill of violent mob encounters. He writes of occasions in which individuals met in pubs, drank and talked, and then left together, *en masse,* heading for the stadium, the train station, or for no particular destination other than a point of contact with another mob. These led in some cases to encounters with other mobs, and in others to violence directed against innocent individuals, even families, who happened to come into contact with the fringe of the mob. His accounts range from the amusing to the horrible, raising questions of many kinds, and supporting the inclination to condemn such phenomena in the strongest moral terms.

### A. When All the Members Do Wrong

Consider first an attribution of blame directed at two mobs of soccer supporters for violence that resulted in the hospitalization of mob members. One might well intend to be making a distributive claim, thus attributing blame to all the members of each group, including the victims. Whether or not one has evidence that all are to blame, one may intend to attribute blame to all, and may have such intentions for several possible reasons. Perhaps one does not know the names of all the mob members; perhaps one thinks that all were involved in the violence; or perhaps this is a convenient and unambiguous way to assign the blame.

Now suppose that one of the mobs is effectively rounded up by the police and brought in for arraignment. And suppose that two individuals claim that they were not part of the mob, but just happened to be walking along with it, supposedly unaware of what might happen. The question for the authorities is whether they deserve blame with the rest, and whether they really were part of the mob that is to blame.[3] Such questions might be answered by questioning other mob members to determine how these two acted in the midst of the mob, what they said, etc. And in establishing the likelihood of whether they were members of the mob, the answers to such questions could also establish whether or not these individuals deserve blame along with the rest. For in attributing blame to the mob, one might be attributing it to all and only the members of the mob.

Would participation in the mob constitute evidence of partial blameworthiness for its violence? Participation in the mob would be participation in what May has called the "solidarity" of the mob, and its "pre-reflective intent." That is, participation in the mob is acceptance of the mood, sentiment and a likely place within the mob in some forthcoming action. Testimony by other mob members could present evidence of one's acceptance and sharing in this solidarity. It is not simply the fact of membership which would provide evidence of individual blameworthiness. Rather, it is acceptance of that which mob membership involves that reveals the extent of one's individual responsibility.

Evidence of mob membership in such a case is importantly different from evidence of membership in an organization. Proof that one is a member of the organization does not necessarily prove prereflective intent to contribute to a wrong attributed to the organization. A lab technician working for a company may have absolutely no idea or intent of any kind whatsoever to contribute to some unethical policies of the marketing division of the company. This fact is well accommodated by the five conditions. However, membership in a mob may be sufficient to implicate all mob members if those who gather to form it accept a set of values or purposes which are directed at some unethical purpose. Recognition of this fact may be embodied in one's intent that in blaming the mob, one is attributing blame to all of its members.

## B. When Some of the Members Do Wrong

One may also blame a mob for the actions of a few of its members. Consider the plight of a man described by Buford who, walking with his family, encountered by chance the fringe of one of these mobs of football supporters.   He was, quite gratuitously, attacked by a few mob members; smashed across the face with a heavy metal bar, then kicked and trod upon in full view of his family, which he had hastily jammed into their car.   Buford saw this happen, and heard the sound of ambulances arriving soon after.[4]

Imagine, then, the man's discussion with the police the next day in the hospital in light of the fear, pain, and anger he no doubt felt.   Imagine his inclination to blame the mob of football supporters for his plight.   How does one best interpret the meaning and reference of such blame?

In blaming the mob, the man may well be blaming not simply the handful of individuals who, quite unprovoked, brutally attacked him.   He may, instead, attribute this beating to the mob in general.   If so, there are two likely interpretations of the intended reference of such a claim.   He may intend, on the one hand, to be attributing the blame to all the individuals in the mob.   Or he may, on the other hand, blame the mob itself but not all of its individuals. He might, in the interest of accuracy, admit that not every individual in the mob is to blame, while granting that the mob is still properly blamed.

Given the fact that he was attacked by only a few of the mob members, what evidence could there be supporting the attribution of blame to each individual in the group?   It might well be the case that the individuals who attacked as they did would not have done so had they not been in the presence of the mob.   They may well have acted as they did due to the influence of the mob they had joined, and because they felt that it condoned such behavior. Indeed, as Buford shows, these football supporters came together to form mobs for the precise purpose of participating in mob violence, expressing openly to one another, even before they had joined together, the hope that "it will come off," that the violence will occur.[5]   The mob members who did not actually attack the man may have contributed, by their willing presence, to the violent acts of a few.   Because that presence was no accident, and because of the intentions they clearly had, they may all deserve moral blame for their causal contributions to the result.   The attribution of blame to each individual could be established as the evidence came in.

Suppose, on the other hand, that the victim admitted that not all mob members were to blame, pointing out that several had tried to pull back the aggressors.   Could it make sense for him to attribute blame to the mob, given such circumstances?   It certainly might.   For he might mean, first, that most of the mob members deserve blame, or second, that the mob, thought of as a whole, deserves blame.

He might, first, explain that the mob is to blame because some of the members of the mob are to blame.   Why would one say, apart from carelessness, that the mob is to blame if one meant in reality that only some of its members are to blame?   There could be a number of possible reasons.   First, one might believe that further examination of the case would likely reveal that most of the mob members are to blame.   By saying that the mob is to blame, one encourages others to think that many in the mob are likely to blame. One encourages further inquiry into this possibility. Second, one might believe both that some are to blame and that some are not, and in addition that it was because of the presence of typically mob-like mentality that those who are to blame are in fact to blame. So one says, "The mob is to blame," meaning that blame attributed to some of its members is appropriate given their mob mentality. Third, one may intend blaming of the mob to be blaming some of its members because one wants to make a dramatic statement, but thinks that some of the members were probably not to blame.

The second meaning of a statement asserting that, "The mob is to blame" while recognizing that some of its members are not could be that the mob should be thought of as something similar to a moral being, and that blame can be attached to it. Since it is made up of morally responsible individuals, and they could and should have acted responsibly, and deliberated, there could and should have been an internal decision-making structure among them. But the mob members chose not to deliberate in any such responsible way. However, because they had the potential to form and exercise such a structure, and the solidarity facilitating it, and because they had a duty to do so, the mob can be considered as if it were a moral person although in fact it was not. In blaming the mob, one can thus leave it unclear as to whether or not any individuals are to blame. One may intend to blame the mob as a unitary thing with decision-making capabilities (although not in fact realized or exercised). This blame may reflect the fact that those capabilities should and could have been exercised, although in fact they were not.

Whether or not such intended meanings are plausible or well supported by the evidence is quite another question. The important point is to acknowledge the diversity of them in relation to various purposes and kinds of available evidence. Such meanings and reference should not be ruled as necessarily implausible by some sharp ontological distinctions between organizations and other collectivities or by sharp distinctions among various kinds of the latter. Attributions of blame directed at all collectivities should be judged on their own merits, in light of their intended meaning, reference and the available evidence. Some may be intended distributively, and some nondistributively.

## 7.2 Collective Blame Without Solidarity

To blame a mob is often to blame a group of people brought together by a relationship of solidarity. Such relationships occur in widely varying degrees. Yet blame can be meaningfully attributed to a collectivity when such solidarity is largely absent.

Joel Feinberg has suggested a case that can be adapted to illustrate how blame can be attributed to a collectivity that is little more than a group of people and that is largely lacking in solidarity. Suppose that a thousand strong swimmers are sunbathing on a beach, and Smith, who is drowning off shore, calls for help. Everyone hears him, but no one takes any steps to rescue him, and he subsequently drowns. In what sense might one say that the crowd is to blame for Smith's demise?[6]

There are, of course, two questions here. First, what might one reasonably mean in making such a statement? And second, what interpretation of such a claim is best supported by the evidence? In this case, both questions are best answered by a statement supporting a distributive interpretation to the effect that "All the sunbathers are to blame." If, in fact, each one of the sunbathers could have saved Smith, each one had a duty to try to do so, and each one chose not to, then the evidence would show they are all to blame.

It is not, however, impossible to imagine circumstances in which a non-distributive interpretation is also called for. Consider the point of view of one of the sunbathers who is accused by Smith's relatives of sharing guilt for Smith's death. That sunbather might well respond that blame falls on the group, but not on all the individuals, and that blaming the group need not be thought of as blaming all the individuals. This sunbather might then present a case for one's own complete innocence, based on lack of lifesaving skills and the belief that a lifeguard was somewhere on the beach. Yes, the group is surely to blame, for it could well have prevented the drowning. But not everyone in it shares the blame. Some surely do, and that is sufficient to warrant an attribution of blame to the group. But such an attribution can refer in the end to nothing more than some indefinitely identified number of individuals in it. Since we do not know just who they are, but are sure there are some, we direct blame at the group, intending the claim in a non-distributive sense.

Still, the presence or absence of solidarity in the present case is largely irrelevant to the question of whether or not the attribution of blame is distributive. That question is best answered in light of the intent and purposes of the speaker.

Feinberg has suggested another case which also appears to be an example of attributing blame in a nondistributive way to an unorganized collective. This is the case of the passengers on a train car who were held up and robbed by Jesse James alone, without help from other desperados.[7] In this case, James stood at the front of the car brandishing a gun and demanded that all the passengers hand forward their valuables. They apparently did so, and he escaped successfully.

There may well be reason to blame the group of passengers for not having resisted James, even though none of them in particular are known to deserve blame for not having done so. What might excuse any specific individuals from blame is, presumably, the fact that if any one had tried to resist, James might well have shot the person. Since no one has a moral duty to risk one's life to resist a robbery, no individuals on the train can be blamed for not resisting.

But if they had acted together as a group, the passengers could well have resisted with a very high chance of success, due to their large numbers. Perhaps the group was unnecessarily timid and deserves blame for this fact. Such blame appears to be best interpreted as nondistributive.

By intending the blame to be nondistributive, one might mean that some, but not all of the passengers are to blame. Thus, one might hold that the father sitting in the tenth seat with his two children is surely not to blame, since he lacks any duty to oppose James and risk the lives of his children. But one might blame the group in the firm belief that many in it, although as yet unidentified, could have resisted successfully. Whether or not such blame is supported by the evidence, it may be coherent and reasonable to blame the group and intend it in such a non-distributive way.

It seems clear that attributions of blame to nonorganized collectivities can be interpreted meaningfully as either distributive or nondistributive, depending on one's intent and the circumstances. The level of solidarity may be irrelevant to one's intended meaning. One need not distinguish among kinds of collectivities in order to clarify such meaning, reference or the plausibility of the claim.

# Part II  Blaming Individuals, Groups, or Organizations?

There is a set of additional questions that were raised earlier, and postponed, and that can now be addressed. These are the questions of competition between the blaming of organizations and the blaming of other collectivities. That is, why might one be inclined to blame an organization instead of a group, or vice versa? It is argued in the next two sections that such decisions are often made on pragmatic grounds, for specific purposes, and that even the evidence selected to support them may be determined by pragmatic considerations. There may well be, in such cases, no objective reasons why it is preferable generally to blame one kind of collectivity instead of another.

### 7.3 Should We Blame the School, the Team, or the Individuals?

In Midland, Michigan, at about 12:30 AM on October 4, 1991, a car containing two high school students careened off the road and crashed into a tree, injuring the driver and killing the passenger. The two had been at the house of a member of the boys' high school soccer team, together with the other members of the team, having a party at which a keg of beer was consumed illegally by boys who were younger than the legal drinking age. The consumption of alcohol by these team members had broken training regulations as well as the law. The party had taken place without the permission or knowledge of any adults.

Before leaving the party, the driver of the car had assured his friend that his judgment and abilities were not seriously impaired, and that he could drive safely. The friend had accepted this assurance, although expressing some reservation. Others had realized at the time that the driver was staggering under the effects of his consumption, but they had not intervened.

Subsequent investigation of the accident and the party revealed that the idea of the party had first been mentioned by the players at one of the team practices. In addition, all and only the members of the team had been present at the party. Although some had not consumed any beer, they freely admitted guilt for condoning and participating in the party, and for not having taken more responsibility for the safety of their friends. Indeed, they expressed a willingness to accept whatever punishment was given to their friends.

The accident and ensuing reactions to it threw the city into a turmoil of controversy, raising a host of important and difficult questions of blame and policy which were discussed by parents, school administrators, the Board of Education, and citizens informally, at meetings and through letters to the editor of the local paper. One early official reaction by the school administration was the suspending of the team from playing any further games in its schedule for the remainder of the year. The stated rationale for this reaction was that the players who had broken training rules should suffer the consequences as dictated by pre-existing school policy. In the weeks that followed, a protest arose from parents and other members of the community. Some argued that the penalty was too harsh. Others insisted that it was only because of the accident that the entire schedule of games had been suspended. Had the boys been caught drinking and the accident not occurred, they maintained, the suspension of players would have lasted no more than a month. Thus, the team members were being punished unfairly due largely to bad luck. Others charged that the rules permitting punishment of the team and its players were unfair because no such rules applied to members of other high school clubs and organizations. Still others claimed that it was inappropriate for the school to have specific penalties for illegal consumption of alcohol. Since it is illegal, it should be a matter left to the law. The school staff should cooperate with the police, but not impose separate penalties.

These and other charges and arguments were answered with counter-arguments, as discussion of the moral questions churned into a maelstrom of controversy. After a month of suspended play, the soccer team was finally allowed to resume its schedule. The Board of Education appointed a committee to study the question of school rules regarding alcohol consumption. Those who could picked up the pieces and continued on with their lives, emotionally scarred as they were by painful events whose details were known, but whose meanings were complex, unclear, and unsettled.[8]

The question of relevance to this study is that of who is to blame, and why one might blame individuals, groups, or organizations associated with the tragedy. That the driver, the passenger and the team members are partly to blame, even if to varying degrees, seems clear. But what of the team, the school and, finally, the town itself? There may be motives to blame each, and evidence supporting such blame. There is, no doubt, plenty of blame to go around.

The parent of one of the players who did not drink might well be inclined to blame the team. In the eyes of this parent, the team was to blame for the trouble in which the boy found himself. It was not simply a number of individuals who compromised the reputation of the boy, but that particular soccer team. Of course, one might argue, it was not the team which was at the party, but simply its individual members. To this, the parent might reply that those boys were there because of plans made at team practice and because of the existence of team solidarity. As a result, it is not misleading to attribute blame to the team for the party and its results.

In leveling moral blame at the team, such a parent might intend to be treating the team as an organization capable of internal decision-making. Or such a parent might be intending the referent of this blame to be all the members, excluding the parent's son. Such intent is both understandable and possibly supported by some of the evidence.

The local newspaper editorial writer might be inclined to blame responsible individuals such as the coach, and the school as well. The coach should know the players well enough to detect the inclination to engage in such illegal behavior. The school administrators should be encouraging athletic coaches to keep careful track of the activities of the players, ensuring that they do not break training. The school itself should encourage an atmosphere of honesty, lawfulness and purity of body and spirit. The widespread disregard of these values within the school indicates something profoundly wrong.

Such an editorial writer might intend to be blaming the school as a decision-making entity. Or the writer may intend to be blaming an indefinite number of people within the school, or even to blame everyone in the school. There may well be evidence that many more people in the school could have done far more than they did to foster an atmosphere less conducive to such lawlessness and its resulting tragedy.

A certain town resident with a philosophical bent, writing to the newspaper, might be inclined to blame the whole community for the disaster. Such an individual might argue that it occurred because of a widespread complacency regarding illegal drinking by minors. This individual may attribute blame in a distributive or a nondistributive sense, and also to an organization as if it were a moral person. Intended distributively, one might attribute a sort of universal guilt shared by all in the community who knowingly turn their backs on these serious problems. Nondistributively, one might attribute guilt to the community, unsure of exactly who is most to blame, but intending to blame some indefinite number of citizens within it. Moreover, the town may be blamed for the failure of its decision-making mechanisms to address this ongoing problem.

Some citizens may argue persuasively that blame is not the important issue. Rather, the town should seek to formulate policies and procedures that ensure justly the prevention of such lawlessness and tragedy in the future. Policies that single out athletes for special rules and penalties are profoundly unjust and encourage disrespect for school rules and community sentiment. The penalties resulting from such policies are simply an idle form of unjust blaming.

The parents of the victim may well be inclined to attribute blame, even if only privately, alone, or to each other. But in their case, such blame may well be directed, at one time or another, at the full gamut of plausible objects including the driver, the team members who encouraged the drinking in various ways, the coach, the principal of the school, many students in the school, the school itself, the Board of Education, and the whole town. Such blame may be intended in any number of possible ways at various times, and may well be supported by such evidence as that described above.

The diversity of such blame, its motives, evidence, and the viewpoints on which it is based indicate a pragmatic dimension of blaming. The objects at which people direct blame are selected in light of people's purposes and motives, not simply because a case can be made to support such blame. The parent of the nondrinking team member is inclined to blame the team because this blame best serves the purpose, dear to the mind of that parent, of accounting for the son's besmirched reputation. The editorial writer seeks to direct the leaders of the community to take steps to prevent such events in the future. So this writer blames the school, directing public attention to a broad but manageable area in which appropriate changes can be made, where such changes would have realistic promise of preventing further such disasters. The writer of the letter to the editor, on the other hand, is more likely to direct blame at the community because this writer views one's task as that of social critic. Those who oppose school penalties may oppose the propriety of all blame due to their convictions that justice should be the primary concern in such cases.

The parents of the victim are driven largely by their grief, working it through by exploring different avenues of blame in their own minds. They may perhaps move from blaming one individual to another, from blaming one group to another as they review over and over in their minds various sides of the question, "Why?" Having no clear, single purpose in blaming, they may not persist in blaming one particular individual or group, nor in any one distributive or nondistributive intent of such blame. Nor may they, finally, find any such blame very satisfying. Neither attributing blame nor establishing blameworthiness may relieve the grief of personal loss.

Cases such as this present little reason to think that organizations or other collectivities are blamed simply because they are believed to be in fact blameworthy. This case reveals that the inclination to blame and the targets of such blame may well be determined to a significant extent by pragmatic considerations. The particular form blame takes may be determined by one's motives and purposes as well as the available evidence.

## 7.4 The Pragmatic Relationship of Purpose, Evidence, and Blame

If blame may be attributed partly in response to human needs, so may be the selection of the evidence adduced to support it. There may well be a wide array of evidence supporting the blameworthiness of different parties in a given case. Yet, many who blame in such circumstances direct their blame at a single target. They seem not to search about to find an object of blame that is best supported by the evidence. Rather, they consider the question of whether the evidence available to them supports a particular attribution of blame. If it does, they may be inclined to attribute such blame accordingly. Rather than attributing it to all those whose blame is supported by the evidence, they may well direct their blame at a particular object. They may cite as evidence that which supports their views, ignoring the import of further information supporting additional claims of blame.

Consider, on the other hand, the impartial observer, who, regarding the car accident, seeks to determine who is most to blame. There is an important sense in which such an approach is unenlightening and futile. Even if it does arrive at an answer, the result may not eliminate other candidates.

Suppose one concludes that the driver of the car is most to blame. There is plenty of evidence to support such a view. But neither does it eliminate from the range of plausible blame the team, the coach, the school or, in some broad sense, the town. Such a conclusion does not reduce or overshadow the plausibility of claims that these other candidates are to blame. Nor does it show that people who blame the other candidates should redirect their blame to the driver. It is their purposes in blaming which, together with some plausible evidence, reveals the significance and plausibility of their claims. To the extent that those purposes are important and justifiable, and there is evidence to support their views, their attributions of blame may well be plausible.

It is, then, not simply evidence of the actual blameworthiness of some individual, group or organization which decides the cogency of such blame. Rather, evidence of blameworthiness is itself significant to the extent that there are legitimate purposes to blame the individual, group or organization named. As blameworthy as the evidence may show one to be, the absence of significant purpose to blame such a party may be sufficient to obscure the significance of such evidence.

There is, then, an important sense in which blameworthiness, like actual attributions of blame, has a pragmatic, and thus only a partially objective basis. Evidence is, of course, essential for both. To blame without evidence of blameworthiness is specious. But just as one will not bother to blame without having justifiable purpose to do so, evidence of blameworthiness is of little significance unless one has significant purpose to blame. The evidence we cite to support a claim of blameworthiness is selected in part because it helps us achieve our purposes in blaming.

## 7.5 A Pragmatic Dimension of the Five Conditions

The pragmatic nature of blameworthiness reveals the limitations of any attempt to formulate necessary and sufficient truth conditions of moral blameworthiness. Not only is such blameworthiness a matter of degree, but so is its significance. A party may be more or less blameworthy, and its blameworthiness may be more or less significant. Any attempt to cite necessary and sufficient conditions of blameworthiness will thus have limited moral value. To know that a party may fulfill conditions of blameworthiness is of limited help in determining whether that party should be blamed. To say that a party is blameworthy but not worth blaming is specious. One can, of course make such a statement, and it is perfectly meaningful. But once stated, the blameworthiness of the party is then set aside. And the evidence of that blameworthiness may have no significance unless there emerges some significant reason to blame that party. Thus, if one were to cite necessary and sufficient conditions for blameworthiness, these would be of significance only if one had a significant purpose to bother to level blame.

Whether individuals, groups or organizations are significantly blamed or blameworthy depends in part on human motives and purposes. The question of which to blame cannot be decided simply by determining whether organizations, groups or individuals fulfill some set of necessary and sufficient conditions for blame. This conclusion reflects upon the five conditions formulated in 2.5. Their implications are also limited. They must be tempered by this further pragmatic element.

It is worth considering whether to formulate an additional condition specifying this pragmatic element that may be added to the five in 2.5. Such a condition might state:

> Some significant moral purpose is served by naming the organization as blameworthy instead of individual humans, some group of people, or some other organization.

There is a sense in which the force of this statement may already be contained in each of the five. That is, there is little point in even considering a morally objectionable matter, a moral duty, or blameworthiness unless these are significant. There is little point in trying to determine if the five are fulfilled in a given case unless the blame one attributes serves some significant moral purpose. It seems likely that the five are normally understood as tacitly requiring such moral purpose. The proposed additional condition would, then, do little more than draw out the meaning which is already present in them. Because that meaning is important, it should be duly noted. But it need not be stated explicitly, since doing so is a largely redundant exercise.

It is worth noting a certain contrast between the implications of this pragmatic dimension and the tone of moral language used to blame groups and organizations. That language appears definite and clear-cut, using qualitative terms such as "blameworthy" or "responsible." However, the cases examined in this and foregoing chapters reveal that qualitative clarity to be illusory. It is comprised largely of rhetorical force and intended meaning, but is not supported by the examination of relevant cases or of the evidence adduced to confirm attributions of moral responsibility and blame. As other writers have noted, the variety of contexts in which such attributions are made in our moral discourse is better accommodated by recognizing that they apply to real cases in degrees.[9]

### 7.6 Chapter Summary

Directed to clarify the similarities and differences between attributions of blame directed to groups and organizations, Part I examines attributions of blame to a mob. Such blame may be intended to be either distributive or non-distributive in meaning and reference. It is noted that mob membership can itself be evidence of individual blameworthiness, but that membership in an organization may, in some cases, offer no such evidence. Although information about group solidarity can offer evidence supporting attributions of group blameworthiness, one may have reason to attribute blame to a group regardless of whether or not it manifests solidarity. It is concluded that the intended meaning and reference of attributions of blame directed at groups depend on the purposes and intent of the attributor as well as the specific evidence available.

Part II examines the conditions under which blame is best attributed to individuals, groups and organizations. People select the target of their blame on the basis of both their own purposes and the evidence available. The relationship between evidence and the target of blame is pragmatic, depending significantly upon one's purposes and motives.

The chapter serves to establish and clarify an important pragmatic element in thought about moral blame. Indeed, the targets of our blame, the evidence adduced in support of it and its meaning and reference depend to an important extent on our purposes in blaming. But there is, of course, no reason to deny that these purposes are also subject to evaluation.

The net result of the chapter is to reveal further the poverty of ontological distinctions as a basis for the study of individual, group and organizational blame. The important aspects of such blame do not reside in the specific natures of these three kinds of objects. The choice of a particular target of blame results both from the evidence available and one's purposes in blaming. We do not intend our blame to have a certain meaning or reference because the object of blame has some deep ontological character. We direct blame when doing so suits important purposes, and there is evidence supporting our claim. Finally, the meaning and reference of such blame can only be understood in light of those purposes.

**Notes**

1. Held, "Moral Responsibility and Collective Action," in *Individual and Collective Responsibility,* ed. French, 115; R. S. Downie, "Responsibility and Social Roles," in *Individual and Collective Responsibility,* 69; Benjamin, "Can Moral Responsibility Be Collective and Nondistributive?," 93-99; French, *Collective and Corporate Responsibility,* 10-13; Mellema, *Individuals, Groups and Shared Moral Responsibility,* 13-16, 24-28.

2. Bill Buford, *Among the Thugs* (London: Secker and Warburg, 1991).

3. *cf.* Howard McGary, "Morality and Collective Liability," *The Journal of Value Inquiry* 20 (1986): 157-165.

4. Buford, *Among the Thugs,* 89-93.

5. *Ibid.,* 79.

6. Joel Feinberg, "Collective Responsibility," in Feinberg, *Doing and Deserving,* 244.

7. *Ibid.,* 248.

8. *Midland Daily News,* Midland, MI, October 5 - November 6, 1991.

9. See note 7. in chapter one.

# Chapter 8

---

# Punishment and the Five Conditions

One of the most important purposes of blaming an organization, group of people, or an individual is to establish the justifiability of punishment. The analysis of the five conditions for attributing such blame may thus have implications for judgments about the propriety of punishment. Examination of such implications in the present chapter reveals the consistency of the five with our intuitions about punishment and its justification. In addition, the principles at the heart of the five, particularly dependency and sufficiency, are reflected in various relationships among individuals and organizations in contexts of punishment. The reasons why this is so offer added support to the analysis developed through the five.

The study of relationships among individual and organizational blame and the justification of punishment confirms the descriptions in chapter seven of the relationships among organizations, individuals and groups. It reveals that in contexts of punishment as well as blame, organizations differ from groups mainly in degree. Punishment of organizations and groups affects individuals in similar ways. And the justification of punishment of both organizations and groups is properly evaluated in light of the effects of the punishment on individuals, and their likely blameworthiness.

## 8.1 Punishment, Deterrence, Consistency, and Compensation

It is essential to understand from the outset the differences among various justifications of penalty. Moral blameworthiness is certainly a necessary condition for justifying punishment, but it is just as clearly not sufficient. One may be morally blameworthy for something, yet not deserve any particular punishment for it. The morally blameworthy practice may be too insignificant to warrant a particular punishment.

Punishment of people who are morally blameless for something is, however, morally unjustifiable. Punishment involves some measure that causes inconvenience or displeasure to a given party, and thwarts the interests of that party. Such measures are unjustifiable unless that party has done something to deserve them. Punishment, then, is justifiable only if it is deserved. And it is deserved only if one is morally blameworthy for something. Moral blameworthiness is, thus, a necessary condition for justified punishment, but not sufficient to warrant it.

It is crucial to distinguish punishment from penalties that are leveled for deterrent purposes. It may be justifiable to penalize some party in order to help deter others from certain kinds of practices even though that party is not significantly blameworthy in a moral sense. The party may have broken the law for reasons which are morally excusable, and thus have a genuine exculpatory excuse. However, it may be just to penalize the party in order to let it be known to others that such practices will not be tolerated under any circumstances. Penalties that are justified by reference to their deterrent effects may be referred to as "deterrent penalties" or "deterrence."

A third kind of justification for imposing some penalty on a party is the need to follow precedent and maintain administrative or legal consistency. Such penalties may also be leveled for just, moral reasons, in the absence of moral blameworthiness. It may be more important, for various reasons, to maintain the consistency of policy or the law than to treat a given case as an exception and suspend official penalty. Such justification for penalties may be referred to as "following precedent" or "legal consistency."

There is an important fourth justification for imposing a penalty. This is the purpose of restoring to a first party an equal measure of well-being which was unjustly taken from that party to benefit a second party. Thus, fairness and justice may require an attempt to compensate the first party for some harm suffered as a result of the violation of some moral or legal duty by the second party. Measures of compensatory justice may thus be justified on moral as well as legal grounds, and are often thought to be best justified on both. They may be referred to as "compensatory measures" or "compensation."

Penalties that are imposed on grounds of deterrence, precedence, or compensation may all be justified in the absence of established moral blameworthiness. Such grounds may justify measures that, although viewed as penalties by some, are not justified for retributive reasons, and are thus importantly different from punishment, which refers to retributive measures justified by moral blameworthiness. Of course, a penal measure may be justified by a combination of any of these four kinds of justifications, and possibly more. However, the important point here is that moral blameworthiness is necessary, although not sufficient, only for efforts to establish that measures which count as punishment are justified.[1]

These distinctions are crucial for understanding the relationship between organizational blame and punishment. Observation of them plays a central role in the following discussion which addresses these questions with the help of various examples. The trouble with all realistic examples of penal measures based on retribution is that it is difficult to dissociate them from justifications based on deterrence, legal consistency and compensation. When seeking to justify a penal measure, advocates will typically cite arguments based on several of the four to make their case. Less often in the contemporary world are penal measures justified by retributive considerations alone. However, this is no reason to think that they are irrelevant to serious deliberations. Penalties which are not believed to be in any way "deserved" are often seriously questioned, and reduced in severity. Although retribution alone is probably rarely viewed as sufficient to warrant significant penal measures, and may not be viewed as necessary, it is none the less important in our thinking about penalties of all kinds. And to this extent, retributive rationale can be identified and isolated for examination of its relationship to blameworthiness.

## 8.2 Punishing Individuals, Organizations, and Groups

Before considering the implications of the dependency and sufficiency theses for the justification of punishment, it is important to note certain basic relationships among individuals, organizations and groups in contexts of retributive punishment. These relationships can be understood in light of three main points. First, punishment of organizations affects individuals, and punishment of individuals can affect organizations. Second, punishment of groups affects individuals, whether or not that punishment is directed in a distributive or a nondistributive manner. Third, the punishment of groups and of organizations affect individuals in similar ways. The nature, effects and descriptions of punishments do not reveal a sharply or importantly different status of individuals in groups from individuals in organizations.

### A. Punishing Organizations and Individuals

Consider, first, some ways in which punishment of an individual may affect an organization. Suppose that the president of an investment firm is fined and given a jail sentence as retribution for insider trading. Although the sentence and fine directly affect that individual, they may also, predictably, affect the firm. If that chief executive is the key to the success of the firm, removal of this individual may damage the firm. Moreover, the fine may cause that individual to withdraw a large sum of money from the firm, thus throwing it into financial crisis.

For a judge to maintain that these punitive measures are directed against the individual but not the firm is to ignore the real effects of those measures. It may be true that the measures are directed at the individual and not intended to harm the firm. However, they may be interpreted, understandably, by the firm's employees as retribution against the firm. Thus, the intent of the judge may be one thing and the effects another.

Retribution directed against an organization may also affect its personnel. They may take such retribution personally, and not without reason. For the predictability of the measures may offer support for the view that the personnel are being punished, even if that was not the intent of those instituting the measures.

## B. Punishing Groups Nondistributively

Punishment of organizations may be described as nondistributive in the sense that to fine an organization a million dollars is not to fine each of its personnel a million dollars. Indeed, such a fine may fail to affect in any way the lives of some of the personnel in the organization. Punishment of groups, however, has often been described as distributive in the sense that such punishment has the same effects on each member of the group. Although such points appear plausible, they overlook an important sense in which group punishment may be nondistributive. And they overlook, most importantly, the fact that whether such group punishment is directed nondistributively or not is a largely pragmatic consideration.

Punishment of a group can be understood as punishment of a number of individuals, or as punishment of the group treated as a whole. It seems possible to punish the group in what appears to be a nondistributive way by forbidding it from forming. It appears nondistributive in the sense that to forbid the group from forming is not to forbid the individuals from forming. That is, the punitive measure appears to do something to the group that is not exactly the same as it does to the individuals.

Of course, to forbid the group from forming is to take steps to affect each individual in the group. For each one now knows that he or she must not join with the others for certain purposes. So a punishment described as, "The group is banned from forming" is equivalent to a punishment described as "Individuals 1. . .n must not join together for purpose x." To issue a punishment in nondistributive terms does not eliminate the effect of the punishment on individuals. And the nature of the punitive measures and its effects can be described in either distributive or nondistributive ways.

Given the presence of both options, why might one choose to describe a punishment to a group in nondistributive terms instead of in distributive terms? Why might one choose to ban a group from forming instead of simply ordering each of its personnel to avoid meeting for certain purposes? The answer is that there may be circumstances in which it is more appropriate to describe the punitive measures in nondistributive group terms instead of in individual terms. Something untoward may have happened which is severe enough to warrant punishment of a group by banning its existence, but is not severe enough to warrant any further punishment of individuals. Banning the group from forming may be the punishment that best fits the offense. So the language used is non-distributive in form, although the very same measures may be described in distributive terms.

The nature of a punishment directed at a group may be warranted by the nature of one's intended purposes, rather than by some structural feature of the group. It is not because the group is in fact a unity that nondistributive language is used to describe it. It is because such language is judged as best fitting the circumstances. Once punishment is leveled, it may be described either as punishment of the group or as punishment of each of the individuals, depending on one's purposes in doing so.

## C. The Similarity of Punishing Groups and Organizations

Comparison of the punishment of groups and organizations in light of the effect of such punishment on individuals reveals important similarities between the two. Note, first, some reasons why one might be tempted to stress their differences. For a judge to level a fine at an organization is not equivalent to stating "Individuals *1* through *n* must together produce a sum of money from organizational coffers." Individual number *1* might, after all, leave the organization. Rather, it is those filling organizational roles, whoever they may be, who must produce the money, and it must be produced from the coffers of the organization.

Punishment of a group may require very similar things of each member of the group. In banning the group from forming, each member must desist from doing similar things. However, to ban an organization from forming also requires many different things of each relevant individual. The person who was the president is banned from acting as the president of the organization. Those who were janitors are banned from acting as janitors of the organization. It may thus appear that punishing groups distributes the same kind of mandate to each individual, while punishing organizations distributes different mandates to each.

This is, however, not always true. Banning an organization makes some of the same demands on some different individuals. Thus, it is true for the president and for the janitor that they are not to work for the organization, that they are not to receive payment from the organization, and that they are both to act as if the organization does not exist. Furthermore, banning a group does distribute some different requirements to each individual. It requires of one who tends to be a follower not to follow others who seem to be pursuing the course that the group has tended to pursue. It requires of one who has been inclined to lead the group not to pursue with others such activities which the group has tended to follow.

It might appear that the main difference between punishment directed at groups and directed at organizations lies in the nature of roles. Roles are more clearly defined in organizations than in groups. To describe the effects of organizational punishment on individuals requires reference to its effects on individuals in certain roles. However, because roles are often less clear in groups, punishment of groups may be described in terms requiring the same of all people. Such a picture is, however, not entirely accurate. The effect of organizational punishment on the personnel can be described in ways identical to those that are used to describe the effects of group punishment on group members. For one can state accurately that no one in the organization is to act as the president or the janitor. Of course, the effects of this statement will be different for the former president and the former janitor. The former president will no longer receive a large salary, and the janitor no longer a small one. But punishment of a group affects individual group members differently as well. Some will long for the presence of the group and some will not. Some will pursue former group goals individually and some will not.

The important point here is that there is no sharp distinction between the nature, effects, or justification of group and organizational punishment. That roles are more defined in organizations, that rules and practices are followed more consistently, and decisions are made more deliberately are undeniable. Individuals may relate to one another and perform in some different ways and have different experiences in groups and in organizations. But there are also differences in the relationships, performances, and experiences of individuals in different groups and also in different organizations. There is no basis for arguing that groups are ontologically different than organizations because individuals have a fundamentally different place in each. Individuals have different places in different groups and in different organizations, and these may be understood as differences of degree.

Punishment of organizations and punishment of groups both affect individuals. As the following sections reveal, the evaluation of the degree to which they do so is an important measure of the justifiability of each.

### 8.3 Dependency and Organizational Punishment

Punishment is a means of holding one responsible, and is justified in part by the degree to which one is morally responsible or blameworthy. The relationships between individual and organizational blameworthiness should thus be reflected in the relationships between the justifications of individual and organizational punishment. If organizational blameworthiness may be intended nondistributively and characterized by the dependency thesis, organizational punishment should reflect this nondistributivity and involve a similar dependency relationship. That is, there should be a kind of isomorphism of the relationship captured by the dependency thesis regarding the blameworthiness of individuals and organizations, and a relationship similar to dependency regarding the justification of punishment of individuals and organizations. Examination of examples reveal just such a relationship.

Consider a war debt imposed for retributive purposes by the victor on a nation which lost a war it began. This debt would be paid by the government of the loser and the nation would suffer under the financial burden. Three important points help establish the significance of dependency for the justification of punishing organizations. First, one may punish an organization without punishing all of its personnel. Second, the propriety of such punishment is evaluated in part on the basis of its effects on individuals. Third, punishment of an organization is not retributively justified unless the punitive measures affect at least some of the individuals in the organization.

First, one can take measures described as punishing an organization, although these measures do not punish all of its personnel. Regarding the war debt, not every citizen in the nation would necessarily suffer equally, or to a degree proportionate to his or her blameworthiness for initiating the war. Some may benefit from the imposition of the debt, perhaps working in a job which would not otherwise be available.

Second, the propriety of punishing an organization is determined in part by its effects on individuals. The imposition of the war debt for retributive purposes would be misplaced if none of the "hawks" who favored starting the war suffered from it, or if only the "doves" who opposed the war suffered from it. Indeed, the retributive propriety of the war debt would be evaluated in part by its effect on the lives of those in the nation who are blameworthy for the war. Thus, the justification for a retributive war debt depends in part upon its likely effect on some of the citizens of the nation. If none of the citizens are affected by the debt, or if the wrong ones are affected, the debt may have weak retributive justification.

Third, punishment of an organization that fails to punish any of its personnel is morally gratuitous. To punish the nation without inconveniencing any of its citizens would be vacuous. To punish a corporation by dissolving it completely would be futile if doing so did not significantly inconvenience some of its personnel. Just as it is morally pointless to blame an organization while intending that none of its personnel are to blame, so is it morally pointless to punish an organization unless one intends that some of its personnel are also punished by doing so. Dependency and nondistributivity apply to the punishment of organizations in a way similar to that in which they apply to the blameworthiness of organizations.

## 8.4 Punishing Organizations When Individual Blame Is Fully Known

According to the sufficiency thesis, if the degree of blame deserved by each of the individuals which are blameworthy for something is known, there is no significant moral purpose to blame the organization in addition to or instead of the individuals. If sufficiency is true, then complete knowledge of individual blameworthiness cannot alone justify punishment of an organization. It would be a serious objection to the sufficiency thesis if, on the other hand, complete knowledge of individual blameworthiness can suffice to justify organizational punishment. There are, however, important shortcomings of attempts to provide such justification. A clear grasp of these problems provides further support for the sufficiency thesis and the analysis of organizational blame developed through the five conditions. The following is directed to establish that knowledge of the degree of blameworthiness of all individuals who are blameworthy for some matter may be sufficient to justify punishment of those individuals, but is not alone sufficient to justify punishment of the organization through which their blameworthiness accrued.

Consider again the automobile accident described in 7.3 and assume that it is known exactly which members of the soccer team did what and exactly which are blameworthy and to what degree. Could this knowledge justify the punishing of the soccer team instead of each player individually?

It is important to emphasize at this point that the question is not whether there might be reason to penalize the soccer team by canceling the remainder of its schedule. There certainly might, as the school officials believed. But the justification of penalties must be distinguished from the justification of retributive punishment. Penalties can be justified for reasons of deterrence, legal consistency or compensation. But retributive punishment can be justified only by reasons of retribution, and thus blameworthiness. Any of these other three may offer reason to penalize the team.

The question regarding punishment is whether retribution directed at the team can be justified by complete knowledge of blameworthiness of all the blameworthy individuals. That is, if the blameworthiness of the individuals is all entirely known, is there any reason to take measures described normally as punishing the team instead of or in addition to punishing the individuals individually? And here, the answer is clearly no.

If the blameworthiness of the individuals is known, and it is sufficient to warrant retributive punishment, who or what should be punished? Consider the proposition that it is the team that deserves the punishment. Now why does it deserve this punishment? The obvious answer is that it did something wrong. But if its wrong is comprised of the wrong of its members, as known, then why does it deserve punishment instead of or in addition to them? If they deserve it individually, and we know why, then why punish the organization?

It was, after all, the individuals acting in blameworthy ways to hold the party who are each partly to blame for the accident and deserve punishment for their behavior. Just what sort of punishment do they each deserve? Perhaps they each deserve a fine or a stretch in jail or revocation of their drivers' licenses or public shaming or to be suspended from playing soccer for a period of time. Now if the latter measure is taken, the team will in fact lack players for future games. But such a measure, although describable as punishing the team, is not necessarily the same thing as punishing the team. It is, rather, punishing the individuals in a way which has effects on the performance of the team.

To punish the team would be to do what the school administration did. That would be to rule that the team is not allowed to play. And here is an important difference between punishing the team in this case and punishing the individuals who make up the team individually. To punish the players is to allow the possibility, whether or not it is followed up by anyone, that other students in the school may join the team and play out its schedule while the blameworthy players are each suspended from play. To punish the team, on the other hand, is to ban anyone from playing out the team's schedule.

Again, why punish the team instead of or in addition to its blameworthy players? Why does it deserve punishment for the misdeeds of its players? There is, here, a serious objection to arguing that the team deserves to be punished. For there may be other students in the school who complain that punishing the team causes them to suffer unjustly. By forbidding them the opportunity to play out the rest of the team's schedule, these other students are restricted from an opportunity due to a tragedy in which they had no hand. And this is one sense in which it may well be unjustifiable to punish the team on retributive grounds for the deeds of its players.

Of course, the school administration may be right and there may well be important reasons to suspend the remainder of the team's schedule. Perhaps such a measure would send a strong message to other students and their parents, or to the rest of the community. It may have deterrent effects, set a precedent, or have symbolic significance. But these reasons to penalize the team are not justification for retributive punishment.

The reason that justification of punishment of individuals does not alone justify punishment of an organization lies in the differences between punishing individuals and punishing organizations. Although punitive measures against each may have some of the same net effects, they may also have some different ones. Fining a corporation may have different net effects from fining its board of directors. Capital punishment directed at individuals has different effects from termination of an organization. Retributive justification of one is not sufficient to justify the same kind of punishment of the other.

The point here is not that the team does not deserve punishment. Perhaps it does. One can envision an argument to the effect that it was the very fabric of the team, its values, the relationships among the players, their jokes at practice about drinking and parties, and the permissiveness of the coach and the school administration that facilitated the party and the accident. Such considerations might prove that the team, and not simply its players, deserves punishment. However, these are considerations other than simply the degree of blameworthiness of each individual on the team. That blameworthiness may justify punishment of individuals, but alone does not justify punishment of the organization.

When applied to the justification of punishment of organizations, sufficiency indicates that such justification will require more than simply evidence of individual blameworthiness of organizational personnel. For that which is described as "punishment of the organization" will tend to affect the individuals in it differently from punishment specifically directed at them individually. What justifies one of these kinds of punishment will not necessarily justify the other.

### 8.5 Individual and Organizational Blameworthiness and Punishment

The example discussed in the prior section assumes complete knowledge of individual blameworthiness. There are, however, other examples in which knowledge of individual blameworthiness is incomplete and less clear. Such examples are consistent with the above points and clarify the relationship between individual and organizational blameworthiness and punishment.

Consideration of further cases supports four main points. First, evidence of organizational blameworthiness alone never justifies punishment of individuals. Second, evidence of the blameworthiness of some specific individuals does not alone justify punishing an organization. Third, evidence of the blameworthiness of specific individuals together with certain kinds of additional evidence of the organizational basis of their blameworthiness can, in some cases, justify punishment of an organization. Fourth, evidence of the blameworthiness of some unknown individuals together with additional evidence of the organizational basis of their blameworthiness can justify punishing an organization.

To see that evidence of organizational blameworthiness alone never justifies punishment of specific individuals, consider a case in which there is evidence that an organization is blameworthy for neglecting the safety of its employees. Suppose that such evidence includes unsigned, untraceable memos indicating a willing neglect. This is evidence that some individuals are to blame, but their identity is unknown. Such evidence might warrant attributing blame to the organization, and punishment directed at the organization, such as a fine. But since the identity of the blameworthy individuals is unknown, the evidence fails to warrant punishment of any individuals.

Suppose, on the other hand, that there is evidence that (a) managers A and B are to blame; (b) their blameworthiness accrued and grew through their participation in the organizational network; and (c) they are not alone in their blameworthiness. If these three are true, one may find it reasonable to attribute blame to the organization (in a nondistributive sense). Furthermore, one may have evidence justifying punishment of managers A and B.

In this case, however, the punishment of the individuals is justified by their own fault, not by the fault of anyone else, or of something else, such as the organization. The point is that the very same evidence that confirms an attribution of organizational blameworthiness may support punishment of individuals. But it does so only because that is evidence that also reveals the blameworthiness of the individuals. The punishment of the individuals is not justified in this case by the fact that the organization is to blame. It is justified by the degree of blameworthiness of the individuals. There need be no temptation here to try to justify punishment of individuals due merely to their connection with an organization.

The second point here is that evidence of the blameworthiness of some specific individuals is not alone sufficient to warrant punishment of an organization. Consider a situation in which there is strong evidence that (a) managers C and D are blameworthy for some company policy; and (b) there is no evidence that the blameworthiness of C and D accrued in or developed out of their roles or involvement in the company, or was in any way encouraged by company policy, procedures or culture. In such a case, there is no evidence of the blameworthiness of the organization, and thus no justification for taking measures ordinarily described as punishing the organization. The evidence shows only that individuals are to blame, and that this is blameworthiness for a company policy they originated.

Even a significant variation on the above case fails to justify punishment of the organization. Suppose in addition to (a), that (b) is replaced by (b'), evidence that the blameworthiness of C and D developed as a result of various organizational interconnections, roles or culture. Evidence for (a) and (b') alone cannot warrant punishment of the organization because they fail to show that it is meaningful in any sense to blame the organization for these effects. After all, it could be that no one in the organization could reasonably have been expected to foresee that certain pressures within it would result in the matters for which C and D ultimately became blameworthy.

The third point to notice here is that there are certain kinds of evidence of the organizational basis of individual blameworthiness which can justify punishment of an organization. Suppose that, in addition to (a) and (b'), there is evidence of (c), that others in relevant positions of power in the organization could and should have known of the possible effects of the way things were going, and could and should have done something to prevent them from producing the untoward result in question. This could be sufficient to warrant punishment directed at the organization. Whether or not it is clear just who these others were is irrelevant. It is the fact that they are implicated that could

justify punishment of the organization.  For (a), (b'), and (c) together support
the likelihood that within the framework of the organization, something serious
went wrong which should not have, and which is serious enough to warrant
punishment which may be described as punishment of the organization.  It
warrants punishment of the organization because the origin of the wrong and
the blameworthiness lies within the framework of the organization.

The fourth point here is that evidence of the blameworthiness of some
unknown individuals together with some additional evidence of the
organizational basis of their blameworthiness can justify punishing an
organization.  Such additional evidence should include that specified by (c)
immediately above.  That is, it should reveal that there are members of the
organization who could and should have recognized the likelihood of a
problem, and could and should have taken steps likely to prevent it.  Such a
situation matches that required by the five conditions.  One may argue that it
warrants punishment directed against the organization for the following reasons:
Some individuals are blameworthy; their blameworthiness results in part from
their organizational ties and roles; the blameworthiness is serious enough to
warrant punishment; it is not clear just which individuals should be punished;
punishment directed at the organization is the best way available of ensuring
that the effects of some of the punishment which is due people will reach some
of them, at least in part; and finally, the chance that some of this punishment
directed at the organization will reach some of those who deserve this
punishment is worth the imperfections of this kind of punishment.  Thus,
individual blameworthiness can, together with other evidence, but not alone,
serve to justify punishment which is directed at an organization.

## 8.6 Concluding Observations

In general, it is clear that punishment of organizations and groups are by
nature imperfect measures. Such punishment will tend to affect some members
more than others.  Moreover, they may affect those who do not deserve
punishment, or fail to affect those who do.  The only way to punish in a
manner resolving the twin problems of overkill and underkill is to punish
exactly the blameworthy individuals appropriately.

Lacking evidence to support such precise measures, one may follow any of
three different courses.  One may give up the search for blameworthy parties,
surrendering any convictions about retribution.  One may punish those
individuals for whom evidence is available, allowing others to escape Scot-free.
Or one may assign punishment to the organization or the group, as the case
may be, aware of the limitations and imperfections of such an approach.

There may be advantages to the third option, and they may sometimes be
decisive.  Those people individually most blameworthy, although not
specifically identified, may lie within the group singled out, and thus share to

some extent the reprisal they are due, even if only in small part. The objectionable practice or result in question may be understood best by reference to its organizational basis, not simply by reference to the actions of individuals. In such cases, retribution might be more appropriately directed at the organization than at a few specific individuals.

When penalties against a collectivity are justified by the need to deter, questions of moral blameworthiness are less prominent. Such penalties may be largely justified by reference to the effectiveness of the deterrent measures. The justice of those measures should, of course, be taken into account, and innocent individuals not made to suffer more than warranted by measures necessary to produce a justifiably effective deterrent result. Thus, it would be unjust to execute the one thousand sunbathers of 7.2 in order to deter future drownings.

Although many penalties against organizations are justified by various combinations of arguments based on deterrence, consistency and compensation, retribution may also play a role in their justification. When it does, questions of individual blameworthiness are important. Together with evidence of organizational bases of that blame, it may warrant punitive measures which are directed against the organization, and which have only a little effect on individuals. But organizational punishment which totally lacks any effects on individuals is quite superfluous.

## 8.7 Chapter Summary

The chapter investigates the implications for punishment of the analysis culminating in the five conditions. The first section distinguishes retributive punishment from other penalties based on justifications of deterrence, consistency, and compensation. The second section argues that there is no important ontological distinction between the punishment of organizations and the punishment of groups. Punishment of both may affect individuals in similar ways. What differences there are between punishment of these two are best described as differences of degree.

The third section reveals that the dependency thesis is reflected in the justification of organizational punishment. There is no good justification for measures described as punishing an organization unless the punitive measures affect at least some of the individuals in it. Punishment of an organization could not have its full effect unless it affects individuals within the organization.

Fourth, the sufficiency thesis is also corroborated by examination of the justification of organizational punishment. Complete knowledge of the blameworthiness of all blameworthy individuals cannot by itself provide good justification for punishment properly described as "punishment of an organization." Because of the differences between punitive measures directed at individuals and those directed at organizations, full knowledge of individual blameworthiness can only warrant punishment of those individuals.

Fifth, other relationships between individual blame and the justification of punishment are explored. These reveal that one central consideration allows individual blameworthiness to justify punishment properly described as, "directed at the organization or group." This is the presence of interconnections and purposes of blameworthy neglect that were reinforced within the matrix of the group or organization. We punish groups and organizations because individuals within them have done significant wrong, and that wrongdoing was nurtured by their group and organizational relationships.

Measures designed to punish organizations are imperfect in ways similar to attributions of blame to organizations. Because it is unclear just who are the precise human culprits, such punishment may miss the mark, and be deficient in retributive justice. But one may adopt such measures when one judges the alternatives to be worse. For it is possible, in a given case, that punishment of an organization may give more of the right people some measure of their due than the other presently justifiable alternatives. Combined with considerations of deterrence, consistency, and compensation, it may be better to address penalties to an organization than to give up because guilty individuals have successfully hidden behind an organizational shield.

**Notes**

1. Direct treatment of strict liability has been avoided in the discussion here, although it is referred to obliquely in the discussion of legal consistency, the third kind of justification. Strict liability is not in fact a kind of justification of any penal measures. Rather, it is legal consistency which is the justification of measures implementing strict liability, which is the liability to penalty due to one's violation of a law, in the absence of moral culpability.

# Chapter 9

## Philosophical Issues

Although directed to answer questions about attributions of moral blameworthiness to organizations and other collectivities, the present analysis also sides with certain positions regarding some broad and ongoing philosophical issues. As a result, those who favor opposite sides of these issues may be inclined to object to the analysis on grounds drawn from these general positions. In order to anticipate such objections, it is, therefore, important to understand what about these issues relates to this study, and what about its approach and conclusions favor one side or another of a given issue.

It would be inappropriate to offer arguments supporting any of these general positions as further evidence in favor of the analysis. It should, largely, stand or fall on its own merits. However, brief treatment of some of these issues and the main positions on them does clarify certain important aspects of the analysis.

The analysis is related differently to the debate over methodological individualism and holism on the one hand, and moral realism and antirealism on the other. The first debate pertains largely to the strategy of the argument developed here, and the second to the conclusions of that argument. However, both the individualism of the analysis and its resultant antirealism are moderate forms of these alternatives, and both are based upon and develop a pragmatic approach to the subject.

### 9.1 Methodological Individualism in French and May

Both Peter French and Larry May develop their analyses of the blameworthiness of collectivities in light of the time-honored debate over methodological individualism (MI) and methodological holism (or collectivism) (MH). Although the precise content of MI and MH differ in the writings of various theorists, May and French both cite J. W. N. Watkins's views as central to the distinction. Watkins advocated MI as a thesis about explanations of social processes and events. Accordingly, May cites Watkins's statement that ". . . we shall not have arrived at rock-bottom explanations of such large-scale phenomena until we have deduced an account of them from statements about the dispositions, beliefs, resources, and interrelations of individuals."[1] MH, on the other hand, maintains that statements about social groups, their interrelations and dynamics (which have not been deduced from statements about individuals) can offer fully adequate explanations of social processes and events. MI requires fully adequate explanations of social phenomena to be couched in terms of individuals, and MH allows some such explanations to be developed without such reference. MH allows that social groups and their interrelations can have high explanatory value, while MI denies that they do.

What relevance, then, do MI and MH have for the endeavor to understand attributions of the moral blameworthiness of collectivities of various kinds? Watkins formulated MI and MH in an effort to clarify the nature of explanations in the social sciences. This fact raises questions as to their relevance in developing a philosophical explanation of moral blame directed at organizations and other collectivities. Attributing blame to a collectivity is not the kind of thing Watkins and others had in mind as examples of social processes or events to be explained. They have been concerned more with questions such as why mobs form, why certain prejudices exist, why certain societies go to war, etc. Of course, one might ask, from the perspective of social science, why people do seek to blame organizations. And such questions have been addressed to some extent in prior chapters. But the main goal of those chapters has been to clarify the logic of discourse about collective blame, not to formulate or identify empirical laws of human thought. Thus, there are significant differences between the goals of most philosophical explanations and those developed within the framework of the social sciences. So it is somewhat surprising to find both French and May so profoundly concerned to develop analyses consistent with MI.

French's concern stems from his conviction that MI is incompatible with attributions of moral responsibility to certain collectivities. He maintains that "there is, of course, a class of predicates that just cannot be true of individuals, that can only be true of collectives. Examples are abundant, and surely include 'disbanded' [most uses], 'lost the football game,' 'elected president,' and 'passed an ammendment.' Methodological individualism would be at a loss in responsibility contexts, if accountability ascriptions were of this sort."[2]

But what sort of incompatibility is this? MI does not clearly imply that there are no predicates appropriate to collectivities that are not appropriate to individuals. MI requires explanations in the social sciences to be, in some sense, grounded in or reducible to knowledge about individuals. But the predicates French lists are all explicable, in some general sense, by descriptions of the behavior and interrelations of individuals. That they are formulated to be predicable of collectivities rather than individuals is clear. That this is in any way incompatible with MI is not.

The theory of corporate moral personhood, on the other hand, is indeed more clearly incompatible with some philosophical version of MI. For this theory develops a version of the thesis that moral predicates, when applied to corporations, cannot be explained by reference to the status of individuals within them. According to the theory, the blameworthiness of a corporation is supposed to be as inexplicable by the blameworthiness of its personnel as the blameworthiness of a human is inexplicable by the blameworthiness of its parts, such as its eyes, ears, or brain.

Despite serious limitations of French's theory of corporate moral personhood, the discussion in earlier chapters has not repudiated it in toto. That discussion allows the possibility that one may meaningfully and coherently intend, in blaming an organization, to refer to it as a moral person. It argues, in addition, however, that it can make sense to attribute moral blame to an organization while denying the organization is a moral person. So the question now arises as to whether this analysis embraces MI or, like French, eschews it.

Before addressing the question of the position of the present analysis toward MI, it is worth clarifying Larry May's approach to the issues. May's position is, in some ways, similar to that of the present analysis. However, May takes a decidedly different stand toward MI and MH in general. Although claiming that he repudiates MI, May also repudiates MH, claiming to hold middle ground between the two. May thinks that MH interprets social groups as "superentities" having a reality over, above, and independent of the individuals who comprise them.[3] He thinks MI maintains that "complex social phenomena can be adequately explained by reference only to individuals."[4] But he finds both of these views mistaken.

May, however, grants that MI and MH each contain a kernel of truth. He argues that MH is right in its view that an adequate understanding of certain phenomena requires reference to the nature of a collectivity. Thus, to understand a football game, one must explain what happens by reference to group phenomena such as cohesiveness, division of labor and team spirit, not just the tasks of each individual.[5] He argues that MI is right in its view that collectivities and collective phenomena such as intentions and will do not exist apart from individual persons.[6] So he maintains, in short, that social groups of various kinds are best conceived as "individuals in relationships," and that social phenomena can best be explained by understanding the interactions of individuals in light of those many interrelationships.[7]

Although the analysis developed in this book is largely consistent with the general view of Larry May, it is not consistent with his interpretation of his own view. For the idea that his views differ clearly from MI is, surprisingly, erroneous!   Indeed, throughout his book, May ignores a crucial part of Watkins's formulation of MI.  As May himself actually quotes Watkins, MI allows rock-bottom explanations of social phenomena in terms of, among other things, "interrelations among individuals."[8]   Indeed, that very point has been acknowledged by many of those who have advocated or discussed MI.[9]

To the extent that MI allows that fully satisfactory explanations of social events can be given by reference to individuals in relationships, May's own view is actually a version of MI.  His theory of vicarious negligence clearly embodies the central sympathies of MI in its reduction of corporate responsibility to the vicarious negligence of some corporate personnel.  It is their relationships to others through the complex of corporate interrelationships, including May's concept of apparent authority, which allows one to say that the corporation is negligent.

## 9.2 The Irrelevancy of the Analysis to the MI-MH Debate

The analysis developed in the prior chapters is clearly compatible with May's position on the issues and his version of MI.  The five conditions, including the theses of individual sufficiency and dependency, reveal that attributions of moral blame to organizations, and to other less organized collectivities as well, can be understood by reference to the blameworthiness of individuals.  In order to justify such attributions, one needs evidence of various aspects of the blameworthiness of individuals, and no further evidence of moral blameworthiness.   One does not need evidence that a decision-making procedure has or has not been exercised, or has led to a blameworthy outcome. One need not cite evidence that the collectivity in question does or does not manifest characteristics of moral personhood.  It can make sense to blame an organization if one has evidence that some individuals within it are at least partially to blame for the matter at hand, and evidence that their blameworthiness arose in part as a result of their relations within the organization.  It can make sense to attribute such blame because doing so can help one fulfill certain purposes such as those described in 1.6.

To claim that evidence regarding individual blameworthiness is necessary and sufficient to warrant blaming an organization is not to deny that other evidence may also be used.  It is not to deny that one may adduce evidence of the exercise or neglect of organizational decision-making structures, or of the moral personhood of an organization, or of the moral duties or responsibility of an organization.   Such evidence may well be used to establish a case of organizational blameworthiness. The present analysis is committed to the view that this kind of evidence must, to be efficacious, include evidence of limited blameworthiness of individuals.  That French's actual analyses, for example, clearly do so has been noted in sections 2.2, 2.3 and 3.3. The present analysis is, in this sense, more general than and inclusive of French's holistic view.

The present analysis is not committed to a reduction of organizational blameworthiness to the blameworthiness of individuals. As necessary and sufficient conditions for warranted assertibility, not truth, the five do not offer a complete account of the meaning of all attributions of organizational blame. As revealed in Chapter 4, meaning depends, to some extent, upon the particularities of specific contexts and the intentions of those making such attributions. As such, questions of what a given speaker means are best answered through examination of the particulars of the context. There is little promise in the endeavor to spell out the one, true, universal meaning of all such attributions. Some speakers may be best understood as intending to blame organizations as if they are moral persons, and some may not. The present analysis does not claim that organizational blame is nothing but the blaming of individuals, or that organizational blameworthiness is nothing more than the blameworthiness of individuals. It claims that whatever such blame or blameworthiness may be, whether or not that ultimately can be clarified, a necessary and sufficient condition of such blame being attributed on plausible and morally efficacious grounds is the presence of evidence of limited individual blameworthiness as specified by the five conditions.

For the present analysis to be consistent with MI is not, therefore, for it to contradict MH or to take sides in the general debate whether MH is preferable to MI. In developing this philosophical analysis, the goal has been to explore conditions under which organizational and collective blame make sense, and to clarify the kinds of evidence necessary and sufficient to establish the plausibility of such blame. Unlike the approaches of French and May, this analysis is not developed through a position defined by the debate between MI and MH. Because that debate frames their approach to the moral blame of collectivities, they address ontological questions as if these are prior in importance to questions of the moral blame of collectivities. As a result, they tend to treat the actual human practices of blaming collectivities as less revealing than questions of the nature of organizations and groups. The premise of this study is that organizational and collective blameworthiness can be best understood through the study of the circumstances and human needs that lead people to attribute such blame. When approached from this perspective, MI and MH shed little light on the important questions.

## 9.3 The Present Analysis Does Not Assume MI

A significant objection to the present analysis arises in light of the debate between MI and MH. The compatibility of the analysis with MI may appear to arise right at its beginning. One might argue that the very way in which questions of organizational blame are addressed in Chapter 1 leads inexorably to a view compatible with MI. That is, it might appear that the analysis assumes an individualist perspective from the start and simply follows through that line of thought. As a result, the present approach might seem to eliminate systematically any holist analysis of organizational blame by, in effect, assuming its impossibility.

The present analysis is based on the two theses of individual sufficiency and dependency. If an individualistic assumption is necessary to establish either one, then the analysis is indeed based on individualism as charged. However, review of the argument for each reveals that this is not the case.

The central argument supporting the dependency thesis developed in 2.2 and 2.3 concludes, briefly, that to blame an organization while admitting that no one in it shares any blame for the problem at hand is morally vacuous. That is, such blame cannot achieve the main purposes that are ordinarily achieved by attributions of moral blame. The argument demonstrating this point need not make any individualistic assumption. Whether or not this argument succeeds does not presuppose any claim to the effect that organizational blame can be in some sense reduced to or explained by the blameworthiness of individuals. Whether or not these are true is independent of the question of the moral effectiveness of attributions of organizational blame.

The argument for the sufficiency thesis is more complex and subtle. Here, the inquiry began with the question of why one would seek to establish the blameworthiness of an organization if one had full knowledge of the blameworthiness of all the individuals who are blameworthy for the matter at hand. This question appears to assume that there must be some special reason to seek to blame an organization instead of individuals. If there is no such reason, perhaps organizational blame is spurious and only the blaming of individuals is significant.

A critic might argue at this point that one need have no special reason for seeking to blame an organization. In seeking to identify blameworthiness, one may seek to identify organizational blameworthiness for the very same reason that one seeks to identify individual blameworthiness: if an organization is in fact to blame, then we should discover why. Doing so may help one to serve many important purposes in the future, such as encouraging the organization to change its ways.

An opponent might further develop the objection by taking a Frenchian approach, arguing that there could, after all, be evidence of organizational blameworthiness even before there is evidence of individual blameworthiness. A laxity of company procedures may become evident even before the appearance of evidence of individual blameworthiness. If so, the entire approach of chapter one would appear to be unwarranted. For that approach appears to assume that we first have evidence of individual blameworthiness, and then obtain evidence of organizational connections. But if one first has evidence of organizational blameworthiness, one might argue that the blameworthiness of the individuals is simply a separate and different question which one may or may not choose to pursue, depending on one's purposes.

In fact, however, the entire rationale behind the objection is ill-conceived. It is based on a misconstrual of the argument in both of the first two chapters. The argument for the dependency thesis contained in 2.2 and 2.3 reveals the implausibility of an opponent's claim that one could have evidence of organizational blameworthiness before having, or without having any evidence of individual blameworthiness. As argued there and borne out at many points in succeeding chapters, there is compelling reason to think that any significant evidence of organizational blameworthiness will include evidence of individual blameworthiness as well. This is evidence that organizational blameworthiness entails individual blameworthiness.

It is important not to be mislead by the inquiry in section 1.5 that presents an hypothetical case in which it is assumed that we have complete knowledge of individual blameworthiness. The inquiry does not assume that such cases are the norm, or that knowledge of individual blameworthiness is more fundamental or more desirable than knowledge of organizational blameworthiness. The case of complete knowledge of individual blameworthiness is presented in order to help clarify the relationship between individual and organizational blame. The discussion in 1.5 reveals that all significant purposes of blaming can be, in the presence of full knowledge of individual blameworthiness, fulfilled by blaming individuals. Chapter one concludes only that if such complete knowledge is present, there is no significant *moral* purpose to seek to blame the organization. It does not conclude that there is never any need to seek to blame the organization. Rather, 1.6 enumerates eight significant purposes of blaming an organization.

If, on the other hand, one were to reverse the question, one would arrive at an answer further confirming the asymmetrical relationship between the purposes of individual and organizational blameworthiness. Suppose we ask, "Why blame individuals if we have full knowledge of organizational blameworthiness?" The answer is that there may well be very good reasons to do so. As guilty as the organization may be and as well established as this may be, some individuals within it may be so guilty as to deserve to be singled out and blamed for any number of purposes, such as to justify punishment. This is hardly a controversial point, as evidenced, for example, by various legal rulings holding corporate executives criminally responsible for their contributions to certain illegal corporate practices. To blame an organization is not necessarily to be able to fulfill all significant purposes of blaming. There may sometimes be further significant purposes that can be adequately fulfilled only by blaming individuals in addition to an organization.

The question of why one should pursue organizational blameworthiness if individual blameworthiness is fully known is addressed without assuming that one is in some sense more fundamental than the other. Of course, section 1.2

does offer an argument to think that it is clearer to blame an individual than to blame an organization.  And the inquiry does reveal that attributions of individual blameworthiness are capable of fulfilling more purposes than attributions of organizational blameworthiness.  On this basis, one might conclude that individual blameworthiness is somehow pragmatically preferable to organizational blameworthiness.  But even this would be a conclusion, not an assumption of the present inquiry.

The charge that a sweeping individualism has been assumed from the start is belied by the generality and inclusiveness of this inquiry.  It does not rule out the plausibility of an important part of French's holistic analysis.  To allow that people may intelligibly intend their claims of organizational blame as claims of moral personhood is to admit the plausibility of a limited holism.  The present analysis does not deny that some people may intend such claims to have a meaning not clearly compatible with some versions of MI.  Over all, then, the analysis develops a modest but not exclusive individualistic account, based on an approach to specific cases which does not presuppose the truth of a sweeping individualism.

## 9.4 Moral Realism and Antirealism

I presented some early work on the subject of this book to a room full of philosophers at the American Philosophical Association in Chicago in 1985. An interesting comment from a senior colleague was that my arguments appear to show that organizations are not really responsible despite our statements that they are.  The implication was that my position is inherently paradoxical in its appearance to be analyzing organizational blameworthiness.  For the outcome of the analysis was, apparently, that attributions of organizational blameworthiness are in reality nothing but statements about some indefinite number of individuals related through an organizational network.  It is the individuals who are to blame, not some entity labeled "the organization."

The comment was based on sensitivity to an aspect of the distinction between what is known as moral realism on the one hand, and moral anti-realism on the other.  Moral realism may be described as the view that all moral statements are either true or false, and that true ones thus express "moral facts."  Antirealism is the view that the truth or falsehood of moral statements is not knowable on objective grounds, and that the only firm knowledge we have on such matters is that of the evidence that supports them.[10]

The present analysis does not, of course, draw any conclusions about all moral statements.  It is a study of attributions of moral blame to organizations and other collectivities.  To this extent, it does not clearly take sides on the general debate over moral realism and antirealism.

However, the analysis does argue that there are some significant differences between attributions of moral blame to individual humans and to organizations.

Claims of individual moral blame may express all the knowledge we have of moral blameworthiness for a given matter. That is, once we have acquired enough evidence to conclude that an individual is morally blameworthy for some matter, this conclusion may contain the whole of our knowledge about blameworthiness for that matter. Of course, we may always acquire more evidence on the matter. But that additional evidence may simply confirm and reconfirm our beliefs about the blameworthiness of a given individual. Claims of individual moral blame may thus serve as repositories of all of our knowledge about moral blameworthiness, containing the whole truth about the subject.

Claims of organizational moral blame, however, cannot serve as repositories of all of our knowledge about moral blameworthiness. As sufficiency reveals, a claim of organizational blame is a mid-range statement. There can be too much evidence for such a claim, as well as too little. Beyond a certain amount of evidence, no significant moral purpose is served by blaming an organization instead of individuals. Thus, organizational blame is appropriate only in the presence of a certain lack of evidence.

Furthermore, unlike claims of individual moral blame, claims of organizational moral blame are not simply true or false. Most true statements remain true regardless of the amount of evidence one has for them. Statements of organizational blame, however, become irrelevant in the face of too much evidence. That is, the very kind of evidence that at first confirms such statements will justify their abandonment, if too much of it comes in.

There is, in addition, no reason to think that there can be necessary and sufficient conditions for the truth of attributions of organizational moral blame. Even if the five conditions formulated in 2.5 are fulfilled by a given case, it could be reasonable to argue that the organization is not to blame. It could be quite reasonable to argue, instead, that it is more accurate to blame some indefinite number of individuals who likely lie within the organizational framework. It appears that, unlike claims of individual moral blame, attributions of organizational moral blame become implausible in the presence of too much evidence. Such claims are plausible in part because they are practical ways, which help one achieve certain desirable goals, of organizing a certain complex of limited information about individual blameworthiness in organizational contexts.

In the context of the present subject, a realist position is the view that claims of organizational moral blame have no importantly different significance, import or moral meaning from claims of individual moral blame. The anti-realist position is the view that claims of organizational moral blame have an importantly different significance, import, and moral meaning than claims of individual moral blame. The comment made by my colleague placed the results of my analysis squarely in the camp of the anti-realists.

A fully realistic position on questions of organizational blame would maintain that the criteria that one uses to determine if blame is accurately attributed to individuals can be applied similarly to organizations. That is, the same kinds of evidence confirm or disconfirm attributions of the blameworthiness of individuals and organizations. The only difference between the two kinds of attributions is that in one, blame is attributed to human individuals, and in the other blame is attributed to organizations.

French's position represents the realist camp. He argues that corporations are moral persons because they have the same characteristics of moral personhood that individual humans possess. The fact that both are moral persons is what allows one to say of each one that he or she is or is not blameworthy. In doing so, one need not be speaking elliptically about corporations. One may be interpreted as saying that corporations literally are to blame because they are the kind of object which can be blamed, exactly as humans are.

The present analysis, on the other hand, makes no such claim. It does not argue that organizations are moral persons (although it allows one to view them this way), nor does it argue that attributing moral blame to an organization is always doing the same thing as attributing it to a human being. To establish the blameworthiness of an individual, there is no consideration of whether anything analogous to the parts of the person are in any way responsible for anything. The person is treated as one indivisible entity, whose moral blameworthiness is determined only by consideration of what that person did, did not do, could and ought or ought not to have done. The five conditions, on the other hand, treat an organization as a composite that includes individual humans as elements.

If charges of individual blame are ways of organizing and describing our knowledge, charges of organizational blame might better be described as ways of organizing our lack of such knowledge. If claims of individual blame can serve to capture the whole moral truth of a situation, claims of organizational blame cannot. Where claims of individual blame may serve as goals of inquiry, end points capturing a final moral appraisal, claims of organizational blame may not. To this extent, the present analysis provides an antirealist view of organizational blame.

### 9.5 The Intuitive Advantage of a Moderate Antirealism

Some may view the antirealism of the present analysis as a disadvantage. There is, after all, a certain basic intuitive appeal to any realist position. This appeal is based in part on the rhetorical force of the language of organizational blame. To say that the organization is to blame appears to have the same force as saying that a human person is to blame. It is naming one entity and predicating of that entity the moral property of blameworthiness. To attribute such blame appears to be doing the very same kind of thing one does when one attributes blame to a human. That is, one appears to be saying that the property of moral blameworthiness can be attributed to the organization for the same reasons that it can be attributed an individual, and that attributing it to an organization is attributing to that organization the same thing that one attributes to an individual. The only difference between the two attributions is in the nature of the object to which it is attributed. One is a human and one is an organization.

Such considerations are forceful and lend strong appeal to French's analysis that there is important common ground between attributions of individual and corporate moral blame. French's argument that corporations have moral personhood in the same respect and for the same reasons as do individuals makes an appealing case for the view that both kinds of attributions have the same significance, import, and moral meaning. Prior to a careful scrutiny of its ontological and philosophical basis, French's realism on this issue has a powerful intuitive appeal.

The position developed out of the present analysis, on the other hand, may seem intuitively less appealing. It may seem less obvious that in order for it to make sense to blame an organization, some individuals in the organization must be to blame. It may seem less obvious that to support an attribution of blame to an organization, one must have evidence of individual blameworthiness. It may also seem less obvious that organizational blame serves no significant purpose in the presence of complete knowledge of individual blameworthiness. The five conditions indicate that questions of individual blameworthiness are more intimately connected to questions of organizational blameworthiness than is immediately apparent. As such, the present analysis might appear, to the casual observer, to be the intuitively less appealing of the two views, the more complex to state, and the one requiring perhaps more extensive argumentation in support.

French's denial of the dependency thesis, however, results from little more than the intuitive appeal of the claim that a corporation can be to blame although its personnel are not. His implicit claim to have clarified the one coherent basis for blaming corporations precludes without argument an individualist interpretation such as that based on the five conditions. His realistic position is based on an unsupportable bifurcation between two supposedly distinct kinds of collectivities. As argued in the prior chapters, his position fails to account for the plausibility of a broad range of evidence and intended meanings which characterize many contexts surrounding attributions of organizational blame.

Despite the complexity and subtlety of the five conditions, it is important not to understate the intuitive appeal of the sufficiency and dependency theses, and of the overall thrust of present analysis. The analysis is based on several compelling intuitions. Sufficiency formalizes the view that there seems to be little impetus to blame organizations when the blameworthiness of individuals is extensive and well supported. Dependency captures the oddness of blaming an organization if one knows full well that none of its personnel are blameworthy for the matter at hand. The five conditions respond to the fact that most attributions of organizational blame are made in contexts of significant uncertainty as to the blameworthiness of individuals. The analysis clarifies the sense that there is an important evidential relationship between individual and organizational blameworthiness. Finally, the analysis embodies Watkins's important belief that ". . . no social tendency exists which could not be altered if the individuals concerned both wanted to alter it and possessed the appropriate information."[11] By examining and sharpening the implications of these intuitions, this analysis strengthens their force and significance.

Of further importance here is the fact that the present analysis does not contradict the intuitively most plausible achievements of French's work. By allowing considerable freedom in the meaning that one may intend in attributing organizational blame, the analysis allows French to intend, in blaming a corporation, to be blaming a moral person. Although it eschews the basis of French's ontological distinction between types of collectivities, the analysis does not reject entirely the plausibility of the concept of corporate moral personhood. Indeed, whether that notion ultimately stands or falls is of no necessary consequence for the cogency of the present analysis. Its anti-realist character does not preclude the most compelling results of French's realism.

Finally, the antirealist character of this analysis does not imply that blaming an organization may not be similar in some ways to blaming an individual. In allowing one to intend that organizational blame is blame of an organizational person, the analysis allows the possibility that one may have the same intentions in each of the two acts of blaming different objects.

The antirealism of the analysis is moderate. The outcome is not a dogmatic claim that to blame an organization is to do a certain thing, and never something else. The analysis allows the possibility that in blaming an organization, one may be doing any of a number of different things. Some are like blaming an individual human person, and some are different.

Rather than dictate what one means when blaming an organization or other collectivity, the analysis encourages self-reflection by those concerned to attribute organizational blame in earnest. It counsels one to examine one's intentions, their justification, and the evidence available in order to arrive at a clear understanding of the intended meaning of one's claim, and an assessment of its plausibility.

## 9.6 Pragmatism

It was pointed out in the introduction that the present analysis is significantly pragmatic in several senses. These pragmatic dimensions raise important questions which deserve consideration. First is the nature of this pragmatism.

This is not the place for a full statement and defense of pragmatic philosophy, which is enormously complicated by the diversity of thought among various pragmatists. The present goal is to put the analysis of the prior chapters in perspective, clarifying some of its philosophical foundation and illuminating some of its motivation.

Some of the spirit of pragmatism can be captured in six general points that reveal more about the direction of a pragmatic investigation than about the fundamentals of a pragmatic position on major questions. In general, most pragmatists hold (1) that questions of the meaning of language are best answered by investigating the practical consequences of the ideas and statements in question. What we know, as first stated in varying ways by Peirce and James, is best understood by determining how we know it, what difference it makes for our lives, and the nature of the evidence that supports it.[12] (2) They maintain that the extent to which an idea fulfills important human goals clarifies that idea and reveals important evidence for or against it.[13] (3) Pragmatists tend to eschew the possiblity of a first philosophy in Descartes's sense, skeptical that a search for some ultimate, universal foundation of knowledge, some set of basic truths in metaphysics, ontology, epistemology or axiology will provide final and fully satisfactory answers to the great perennial philosophical questions.[14] (4) Sharp, fixed distinctions of thought or reality, labeled as dualisms by Dewey, offer little promise of permanent or even adequate knowledge in philosophical or other subjects. Rather, such dualisms often inhibit understanding, clarity, and the development of further knowledge. Pragmatists typically analyze putative absolutes in order to clarify their relative nature, exposing continuity and gradual variation.[15] (5) Pragmatists have neither faith in nor hope for establishing fixed, certain knowledge in any field. They value scholarship that advances inquiry rather than one that purports to have found the final answers to major philosophical questions.[16] (6) Pragmatists are largely empiricists, placing little stock in claims of a priori knowledge. Rather, they tend to believe that the plausibility of claims of supposed a priori knowledge may rest to a significant extent upon the findings of empirical inquiry. Nor does philosophical inquiry provide a kind of knowledge that is independent of empirical findings.[17] In general, then, pragmatists address concrete, practical consequences and human goals in order to dissolve the dogmas, fixed principles, supposed certainty, and final solutions of abstract, closed, fixed intellectual systems, thereby transforming our understanding by promoting reflection and further inquiry.[18]

A pragmatic inquiry into the moral blameworthiness of organizations does not begin with the assumption that the task of an analysis is to identify one true meaning of any statement which attributes blame to an organization. Since meaning is a function of practical consequences and goals, it may vary in alternate human contexts. A pragmatic inquiry begins by examining the goals and practical consequences of blaming an organization. This is exactly the enterprise of the first two chapters.

The first chapter clarifies the purposes of blaming an organization. It reveals that a major purpose for blaming organizations arises in the presence of a certain limitation of the available evidence for blaming individuals. What motivates the inclination to blame the organization is a shortage of evidence of individual blameworthiness. The sufficiency thesis reveals that the absence of this shortage obviates any significant purpose for blaming an organization.

A pragmatic analysis is one that is firmly based on a study of practical consequences. There are a number of different interpretations of what pragmatists refer to as "practical consequences." The practical consequences of a statement may be the behavior to be expected from those who believe the statement to be true. They may be the practices which the statement, if true, serves to justify. They may simply be what people do if confronted with such a statement. They may be what people do to obtain evidence to confirm or disconfirm the statement. Virtually all of these interpretations of practical consequences are addressed at various points in the analysis. The last one is, in particular, the focus of attention in the second chapter supporting the dependency thesis.

The second chapter investigates a practical consequence of any act of blaming an organization. This consequence of blaming is the search for evidence to justify it. The minimal amount of evidence needed for one to have plausible reason to blame an organization includes evidence of the blameworthiness of some of the individuals of the organization. The argument supporting the dependency thesis has an important pragmatic dimension. It argues that there can be no significant, justifiable, or typically moral purpose served by blaming an organization unless there is evidence that some of its individuals are partly to blame as well. The first two chapters thus support the view that the blaming of individuals, organizations, and groups each require evidence that some individuals are to blame. This evidence of individual blameworthiness is thus essential to all justifiable and characteristically moral blaming.

Pragmatists hold generally that the purpose of an act, statement, or idea helps clarify its meaning. If all the justifiable purposes of blaming require evidence supporting the blameworthiness of individuals, then analysis of this evidence should help clarify the blaming of organizations. And this is the justification for analyzing organizational blame in terms of individual blame. That is, the nature, meaning, and justification of organizational blame should be illuminated by examination of the evidence of individual blameworthiness. Examination of that evidence continues through the first four chapters and is developed further in chapters seven and eight.

The pragmatic nature of the analysis stems in part from its avoidance of the assumption that the blaming of individuals is more fundamental in some epistemological, metaphysical, or moral sense than the blaming of organizations or groups. The analysis investigates the purposes of blaming organizations, the evidence necessary and sufficient to support those purposes to a reasonable extent, and finds that these purposes require evidence of the blameworthiness of individuals. This finding neither assumes nor concludes that the blameworthiness of individuals is more fundamental than the blameworthiness of organizations. Rather, real, purposeful human acts of blaming organizations rely upon evidence of limited individual blameworthiness. The argument is that such acts of blaming are incoherent without it. It is an argument about real human purposes and evidence, not about metaphysical reality, truth, or moral reality.

The argument begins by investigating cases of blaming that advance typical and justifiable human moral purposes. Investigation of the purposes of blaming establishes the sufficiency thesis, that none of those purposes are well served when one blames an organization in the presence of full knowledge of the blameworthiness of all the blameworthy individuals. Analysis of the evidence that supports justifiable purposes of blaming organizations establishes the dependency thesis, that it is unjustifiable to blame an organization without evidence that some of its personnel are to some extent blameworthy. Combining the sufficiency and dependency theses with a set of conditions for individual moral blame produces five conditions that are necessary and sufficient for one to have good reason to assert that an organization is to blame for something. These conditions delineate both the minimum and the maximum amount of evidence that constitutes good reason to blame an organization. But they are not necessary and sufficient conditions for organizational blameworthiness. This distinction bears further attention.

Necessary and sufficient conditions are a list of conditions that must be fulfilled for a statement to be true, and that, if fulfilled, establish that the statement is in fact true. The argument indicates that the five conditions must be fulfilled in order for a statement blaming an organization to have good justification. But there is no good reason to think that fulfillment of these conditions is necessary and sufficient for the statement to be true. After all, it is possible that an organization is blameworthy, although for some presently unknown reason. The five conditions delineate the nature of the evidence one must possess in order to be justified in asserting blame, but do not define the conditions for the existence of blameworthiness in some metaphysical sense. The five are conditions of evidence and thus warranted assertibility, not conditions of being.

The five conditions do not state necessary conditions for organizational blameworthiness. An organization may be blameworthy even though we do not have the evidence to fulfill all five conditions. However, if a person trying to attribute blame lacks the evidence fulfilling the five conditions, that person lacks good grounds for attributing blame to an organization.

Fulfillment of the five conditions is not clearly sufficient to establish that a statement blaming an organization is true. The conditions may be fulfilled, and yet it may be false that the organization is blameworthy. Due to the limitation on the evidence required by the five conditions, the blameworthiness may be entirely due to a conspiracy of a small group of individuals within the organization, and full knowledge then would show that there are compelling reasons why the organization does not deserve blame in the case at hand. That is, the evidence at hand may, according to the five conditions, warrant one to blame the organization, although if all the facts were known, such warrant would disappear.

The five conditions are pragmatic in nature, specifying a range of evidence under which certain purposes may warrant blaming. But they cannot be used to establish the certainty of blameworthiness. There is no basis here for some moral dualism distinguishing organizations that are blameworthy from those that are not. The analysis develops a further eschewal of dualism in its repudiation of French's distinction between aggregate and conglomerate collectivities. It is the very justification of the distinction that is flawed, and this is clarified by an analysis of the logic of French's argument alone, independent of the views developed in the first four chapters. The present study takes the human activity of blaming as the subject of analysis, not some supposed sharp differences in the being of organizations.

French's conclusion that organizations are moral persons, but that aggregate collectivities are not, makes the blameworthiness of an organization an endpoint of inquiry, a definitive state of its moral being. French's whole position is based on his argument for necessary and sufficient conditions for the truth of attributions of organizational blame. Yet, to eschew such truth conditions is not, as French would seem to think, to obviate all claims that an organization is to blame. Rather, an eschewal that is developed through the five conditions illuminates both the purposes for attributing blame and the limitations of the evidence that supports such blaming. It opens claims of organizational blame to critical scrutiny from a number of different perspectives.

The present analysis does not offer a definitive clarification of the true meaning of a claim of organizational blame. Nor does it deny Peter French, for example, the right to mean by blaming an organization that a metaphysical person is to blame. He may intend this in meaningful ways and for understandable reasons. But his dogmatic approach implying that this is the main, morally significant meaning such a claim must have is based on his mistaken dualistic ontology of collectivities. French's fixation on the supposed sharpness of this dualism leads him to ignore its pragmatic basis and the range of purposes and evidence for claims that an organization is to blame.

The evidence people actually use to justify blaming organizations together with the purposes of doing so reveal that such blaming is a special way of coping with a moral situation characterized by uncertainty. A full accounting of such purpose and evidence gives little reason to view truth as an important property of such blame. Rather, such statements of blame are best viewed as intermediate, tentative, and imperfect in their significance. They are pragmatic in nature, useful in fulfilling some human purposes, but not delineating a category of moral being.

Finally, statements attributing blame to an organization are best viewed not as endpoints of inquiry. To have satisfied the five conditions for blaming an organization does not establish anything definitive about that organization. Nor does it establish that the job of moral or ethical assessment is over. Blaming the organization may well represent a certain level of knowledge and understanding in a case at hand. But a full grasp of the intermediate nature of such blame paves the way for further investigation, revelations, and reassessments. As a pragmatic way of thinking, to blame the organization is not to utter a final verdict of moral responsibility. If plausible, such blame reveals significant lack of relevant knowledge and the need to pursue a host of further questions about the nature of the organization, its operations, and individual personnel. As the story becomes increasingly known, and one develops a fuller knowledge of the role of individuals, the responsibility of individuals may well supplant the blame of organizations.

**Notes**

1. May, *The Morality of Groups,* 14.

2. French, *Collective and Corporate Responsibility,* 5.

3. May, *The Morality of Groups,* 18-24.

4. *Ibid.,* 15.

5. *Ibid.,* 24.

6. *Ibid.,* 25.

7. *Ibid.,* 5, 9, 17, 23, 24, 27, 40.

8. *Ibid.,* 14.

150 Chapter Nine

9. *cf.* May Brodbeck, "Methodological Individualisms: Definition and Reduction," in *Readings in the Philosophy of the Social Sciences*, ed. May Brodbeck (New York: Macmillan, 1968), 283; Richard W. Miller, "Methodological Individualism and Social Explanation," *Philosophy of Science* 45 (1978): 388; Alan Carter, "On Individualism, Collectivism and Interrelationism," *Heythrop Journal* 31 (1990): 23-38; J. L. Thompson, "What Is the Problem Concerning Social Entities?," *International Journal of Moral and Social Studies* 6 (1991): 71-89.

10. *cf.* Wm. David Solomon, "Moral Realism and the Amoralist," in *Midwest Studies in Philosophy*, vol. 12, ed. Peter A. French, Theodore E. Uehling, Jr. and Howard K. Wettstein (Minneapolis: University of Minnesota Press, 1988) 380-381; H. E. Mason, "Realistic Interpretations of Moral Questions," in *Midwest Studies in Philosophy*, 413-414; *The Southern Journal of Philosophy, Supplement, The Spindel Conference: Moral Realism*, vol. 24 (1986); Peter Railton, "Moral Realism," *The Philosophical Review* 95 (1986): 164-167; Torbjorn Tannsjo, *Moral Realism* (Savage,MD: Rowman and Littlefield, 1990), Chapter 1.

11. J. W. N. Watkins, "Methodological Individualism and Social Tendencies," in *Readings in the Philosophy of the Social Sciences*, ed. Brodbeck, 271.

12. *Collected Papers of Charles Sanders Peirce*, 8 vols., ed. Charles Hartshorne and Paul Weiss (Cambridge, MA: Harvard University Press, 1965-1966), 5.467, 5.468, 5.9; William James, *Pragmatism and Four Essays from "The Meaning of Truth"* (New York: New American Library, Meridian Books, 1955), chaps. 2,6 ; John Dewey, *The Quest for Certainty,* (New York: G. P. Putnam's Sons, Capricorn Books, 1960), chap. 5.

13. Charles Morris, *The Pragmatic Movement in American Philosophy,* (New York: George Braziller, 1970), 20-25; James, *Pragmatism,* 42-49.

14. Dewey, *The Quest for Certainty,* 47-48, 160-163; Morris, *The Pragmatic Movement,* 49, 67; Joseph Margolis, *Pragmatism without Foundations* (New York: Basil Blackwell, 1986), chap. 7; Richard Rorty, *Philosophy and the Mirror of Nature* (Princeton, NJ: Princeton University Press, 1979), 183.

15. Morris, *The Pragmatic Movement,* 123-125; Dewey, *The Quest for Certainty,* chap. 8.

16. Morris, *The Pragmatic Movement*, chaps. 2,3; *Collected Papers of Charles Sanders Peirce*, 1.135, 1.144-1.148, 5.157, 7.108; James, *Pragmatism*, 46, 89-90, chap. 6; Dewey, *The Quest for Certainty*, 193, chap. 9; John Dewey, *Experience and Nature* (New York: Dover, 1958), 7-9.

17. Morris, *The Pragmatic Movement*, 5-7.

18. Kathleen Wheeler, *Romanticism, Pragmatism and Deconstruction*, (Cambridge, MA: Blackwell, 1993), chap. 4.

# Index

## About the Author

Raymond S. Pfeiffer, an islander at heart, pursues philosophical understanding from the standpoint that no person is an island. He teaches regularly in business ethics, medical ethics, the philosophy of science and technology, and introductory courses in philosophy at Delta College, University Center, Michigan, where he is professor of philosophy. He earned his A.B. in 1968 from Kenyon College in Ohio, then served as an officer in the U.S. Navy. His Ph.D. followed in 1974 from Washington University in St. Louis, Missouri, where he studied analytic pragmatism under Richard Rudner, Joe Ullian and Robert Barrett, and ethical theory under Carl Wellman.

He is a member of the American Philosophical Association; the Michigan Academy of Science, Arts and Letters; Amintaphil; and other scholarly associations. He has published philosophical articles on creativity, interpersonal manipulation, feminist philosophy, abortion, collective moral responsibility, loyalty, and teaching. Convinced that courses in ethics should include studies in ethical decision-making, he coauthored, with Ralph Forsberg, *Ethics on the Job: Strategies and Cases*, published by Wadsworth in 1993. He has been teaching workshops on the nature and practice of science for the Dow Chemical Company and is currently pursuing studies in the philosophy of technological research.